To M

Happy trading!

Rob Sinn

BOB SINFIELD looked set to become a full-time out-of-work actor when gag-writing got in the way and kept him unexpectedly employed for 25 years.

He has written jokes for virtually every notable comic performer of his generation from Rory McGrath to Rory Bremner, plus a few others not called Rory. They include Bob Monkhouse, Tracey Ullman, Leslie Phillips, Gary Oldman, Alan Cumming, Stan Freberg, Joan Sims, Maureen Lipman, Lenny Henry, Jasper Carrott, David Jason, Clive Dunn, Tim Brooke-Taylor, Graeme Garden, Paula Wilcox, Eleanor Bron, Joanna Lumley, Roy Hudd, Alison Steadman, Geoffrey Palmer, Lynda Bellingham, Celia Imrie, Richard Murdoch, NOT Rupert Murdoch, Max Headroom and Neil Kinnock. In his spare time, he enjoys name-dropping..

He turned down The Krankies, Little & Large and providing witty ad-libs for *Blind Date* contestants.

At the time of writing (and hopefully at the time of reading), Bob hosts his own weekly radio show on Jazz FM and treads the boards regularly as Lord Buckley the dapper rapper, Squire Haggard the 18th century rogue and Inspector Flint, Scotland Yard's second-worst detective.

ISBN 978-0-9560470-4-5

Please do not nick these jokes. The author has promised to return them to their owners.

THE GAG TRADE

by

BOB SINFIELD

Published by

DOCTOR SIN UK

DEDICATED TO ALL THE COMEDIANS

WHO HAVE DELIVERED MY JOKES

(even the ones who buggered up
the punchline).

CONTENTS

ACKNOWLEDGEMENTS

Special thanks to Ian Brown, Andy Hamilton and James Hendrie who kindly gave me permission to steal their…I mean, to quote from their material - and to John Langdon who doubtless would have done if he'd got round to answering my e-mail.

WHAT MAKES BOB LAUGH

News headlines like...

David Blunkett marries for the second time today.

Doctors to separate conjoined twins from Bangladesh.

Man flies to South Africa to help murder police.

Pope enters Jordan.

WHAT DOESN'T MAKE BOB LAUGH

Anything set in a parallel universe.

Q: How many writers does it take to change a lightbulb?

A: None. They just sit there muttering that if they'd written the bulb, it wouldn't need changing.

THE PARTY OF THE FIRST PARTY

"The biggest problem for off-duty comics is finding something funny to say."

F/X: PARTY ATMOS

GRIFF: Ah Bob, you're in your father's dinner suit.

It was Griff Rhys Jones, greeting me at the BBC's exclusive sixth floor black-tie do. He was right. But how did he know?

GRIFF: Because I'm in my father's dinner-suit. I see your father was a bit bigger than you are. And as you can see, my father's a bit smaller than I am.

The sight of the nation's comedy heroes and heroines in their dicky bows and little black numbers made entertaining viewing, especially in the case of Jasper Carrott whom I'd never seen out of his denims and Nicholas Lyndhurst who, despite having reached adulthood shortly after the last series of *Butterflies*, looked like he'd have been more comfortable in a school blazer and shorts. Only Alexei Sayle and Lenny Henry broke the code by wearing what were known thirty years previously as 'lounge suits', quite stylishly in one case…but not, unsurprisingly, in the other.

The biggest problem for off-duty comics is finding something funny to say. Most are astonishingly ill-at-ease when ad-libbing and that night I began to wonder if we writers had only been invited to provide the stars with a string of epigrams on cue-cards.

Alexei looked particularly awkward, staring at the floor as if more interested in the carpet pattern than meeting his peers. His wife Linda, clad in comfy slippers with what we now call bling on the toes, was a different proposition altogether. Gregarious and ebullient with a bombastic Scouse delivery, she reminded me of someone, but who? Of course: Alexei's on-stage persona. Here was a painfully shy man making a mint by impersonating his missus.

The Sayle carpet study project reached new depths when the BBC's Head of Variety tried to introduce him to Kenny Everett.:-

ALEXEI: We've met.

…was his curt response before legging it to scrutinise the shagpile at the far end of the room. I can only presume Alexei's objection to Everett was political. In the run-up to that year's election, Kenny had declared at the Tory conference…

KENNY: Let's bomb Russia!

…to rapturous true blue applause, although shortly afterwards Barry Cryer told me Ev had hated the whole event and found meeting Thatcher a chilling experience. At the opposite end of the spectrum, I don't suppose he warmed much to Alexei either.

Come to that, the Two Ronnies didn't exactly hit it off with a couple of the *Not the Nine O 'Clock News* team that night. There was a bit of history here as Mel and Griff from the show had portrayed Barker and Corbett on-air as The Two Ninnies, performing hackneyed word-play routines and cringingly dated musical numbers. At least the Head of Variety had the sense not to try and introduce them to each other, but a lot of judicious body-swerving went on. All the same, the H of V - coincidentally the namesake of Vic Reeves who hadn't been invented yet - revelled in the role of 'mein host' and was, I strongly suspect, a frustrated performer. He was also physically reminiscent of Mr. Creosote, the exploding diner in Monty Python's *The Meaning Of Life*, so we all watched with trepidation lest a passing waiter offered him one waffer-thin mint too many. Needless to say, drink was taken

… and many other substances besides, I shouldn't wonder. Accordingly, inhibitions were swept aside and I was able to see what kind of people celebs turn into when pissed. David Jason's normally precise diction deteriorated into a wistful slur as, almost weeping, he reminisced about the good old days of *Week Ending*, which he'd left all of eighteen months earlier. Still, I'm sure he's not the only one that show nearly reduced to tears (I can say that because I worked on it).

Alcohol had a slightly more ebullient effect on the younger coves. As the official event staggered to a close, Mr. Carrott invited us all to his London residence, The Kensington Hilton, for a post-prandial snifter...because he's filthy rich, you know. At this, sozzled producer John Lloyd piped up in his best Bertie Wooster...

JOHN: Come on, chaps. We're orf to Jarsper's!

Only the straw boater was missing.

Once we were all ensconced in the

Hilton bar, Rowland Rivron and Ade Edmondson took it in turns to get their willies out. At least, I think that's what was happening. Without a microscope it was difficult to tell, but I do remember 'Jarsper' urging Rowland to stick his head up his arse for an encore.

By some stroke of chance, I was still sufficiently in favour with Mr. Creosote to get a second invitation twelve months later. This time, he didn't try bringing Alexei and Everett together and there was no sign of Rowland's penis (probably the cold weather). Some things, though, hadn't changed. At one point, mid-evening, I was just tucking into the buffet when a familiar figure craned round a pillar to inspect me.

GRIFF: Ah, Bob. Still in your father's dinner suit.

Q: Where do funny writers get their ideas from?

A: Funnier writers.

THE CRAPPIEST DAYS OF YOUR LIFE

"My funniest memory of Rory McGrath concerns an outbreak of slapstick at my dad's funeral."

I first met a televison comedy scriptwriter at the age of five and immediately realised we had something in common: he was five too.

Ah, schooldays: the crappiest days of your life. Thirty-nine terms of getting teased, terrorised, torn apart and tantamount to terminated for being too fat, thin, short, tall and/or medium. It's always said in the most cliché-ridden articles about comics that they became funny in the first place to avoid being bullied. But my classmate, Rory McGrath, was funny at five and I don't recall anyone ever bullying him. He was also astonishingly bright. Readers of the book *Bearded Tit* will know about his interest in ornithology (readers of the title alone could probably work it out) but as we graduated from St. John's Primary for Repressed Catholics to Redruth Grammar for Mixed Boys, Rory's polymath status was confirmed. While many of us fled the science lab in panic, seeking refuge in the arms of the Latin master, young McGrath only gave up Physics and Chemistry so he could spend more time with his French and Spanish. AND he could draw!

One thing missing in those days, apart from the beard, was the smut. Fans of *They Think It's All Over* would scarcely have recognised the puritanical streak in the pre-telly McGrath . I put it down to one of two things: God or religion. Our Catholic schooling had more of an effect on Rory (two RC parents) than on me: one RC - and trust me, he could be - and one Anglican. I can remember arguing ferociously with Rory when he expressed a preference for the monastic TV sitcom *Oh Brother!* over the far funnier *All Gas and Gaiters*. If nothing else, you'd think he'd have favoured the latter for its jokes lampooning the Church of England.

But then, I was frequently staggered by how seriously the RCs took this religion lark. Attending the birthday party of another kid in our class, I was fixated by the sight of a holy water font in the hallway. In a '60s bungalow? It just didn't go, love!

Reacting against the primness of his schooldays, Rory McGrath broke out big-time when he eventually swapped Cornwall for Cambridge. Before that happened, we shared many laughs, not least when collaborating on a school revue parody of TV's *Going For A Song* with me as the chairman and Rory as a version of the antiques expert Arthur Negus, an 'antique expert' called Arthur Ritis. Give us a break, we were only twelve.

In our final year, Rory and I went on a school trip to see the poet Ted Hughes at Plymouth Arts Centre. As the coach decanted us, our English teacher (at least I think he was English) pointed to the relevant building and urged us, on pain of expulsion, to be there on the dot of 7pm. We promptly disappeared into one of the city's most disreputable pubs, then another, then a third before emerging into what looked like a much blurrier Plymouth than the one we'd arrived in. Entering what appeared to be the Arts Centre, we announced to the uniformed figure on reception that we'd come to see Ted Hughes. There was a moment of mystification.

UNIFORMED FIGURE [MYSTIFIED]:

Ted Hughes? Is he a cadet?

What was he on about? Cadet?! This man was destined to be Poet Laureate! Gradually, it became clear that what we thought was the Arts Centre was actually the HQ of Devonport Naval Services. We made our excuses, left and hoped we wouldn't be shot for desertion. After that, Ted's performance was a distinct anti-climax: he muttered the poems into his boots and studiously avoided eyeballing the audience all night. Perhaps he should have been a cadet after all.

My funniest memory of the schoolboy McGrath, though, concerns an unintentional outbreak of slapstick at my dad's funeral in 1974. My older brother Michael and I were in the big black car proceeding in a stately fashion along narrow rustic roads towards the graveyard when a purple Hillman Hunter began tailgating us prior to overtaking at high speed. As it did so, we realised the driver was none other than our parish priest, fully vestmented, whose crew comprised two altar boys (Rory and his younger brother Michael), clinging on to the upholstery lest their cemetery excursion proved to be a one-way trip.

Q: How many actors does it take to change a lightbulb?

A: The entire profession: one to change the bulb and the others to shout, 'It should be ME up there!'

2

<u>KEN DODD'S DAD'S DOG'S DEAD</u>

"At 18, Gary Oldman looked 16. Later, he did look 18, but by then he was 36."

Acting? It was all my brother's fault. If I hadn't seen him in the title role of *Billy Liar* at the St. John's Ambulance Hall in 1967, I might never have considered poncing about on the stage as a potential full-time occupation. Of course, he had the sense to stop at amateur acting (where you don't get paid). I had to go and opt for doing it professionally (where you don't get paid).

My school careers adviser, Mr. Balls (great name for someone surrounded by sniggering teenagers) assured me the best way to achieve my vocational goal was to become the manager of a departmental store. As I stared at him, a vital question vexed me, one I dared not voice.

ME: (TO MYSELF) Does he think that wig's fooling anyone?

I knew I'd have to leave my home county if I was to act for a living because there were no professional drama opportunities our side of the Tamar. The only time I can recall any filming down my way was when the BBC shot some exterior scenes for *Poldark* in the summer of 1975. Stupidly, they'd sent down a location scout in mid-January when, of course, he found dozens of deserted villages just right for the eighteenth-century setting, then couldn't understand it when the film crew turned up in July to a county crawling with tourists. I think 'duh' is the expression I'm looking for here.

The following year, as our glorious nation was pulsating to punk rock anthems like *I Love To Love* by Tina Charles, I was slinging my Cornish hook in favour of the Kentish suburb of Sidcup. At first, I thought it was a figment of Harold Pinter's dark imagination. On reaching it, I discovered I was right. Still, the drabness of the town was outweighed by the glorious parkland in which my drama school of choice was set. The Rose Bruford College, called after someone whose name escapes me, was more than just a training ground for actors: it offered classes in Mime, Verse Speaking (or Vocal Interpretation as it was hyped in the syllabus), Textual Studies, Fencing (insert hammer, nails and wooden planks gag here) and something called Theatre Laboratory (there's radical).

The last of these did not, alas, involve shoving the more irritating luvvies into a test tube and roasting them over a Bunsen burner. No, we're talking about something called Theatre-In-Education or trundling round schools in a transit van, a concept hugely of the moment in those pre-Thatcher years. When she got in and more or less abolished state education, T-I-E largely came to an abrupt halt, only to be revived a generation later when *The League of Gentlemen* royally ripped the piss out of it with their naff agitprop outfit, Legs Akimbo.

But back to Sidcup. When auditioning for a place at the college, I hit my first career crisis: someone had swiped my name. I was, according to my passport, Robert Pugh but in his final year at Bruford was a roistering Welshman called precisely the same thing. I didn't fancy my chances at arm-wrestling him for it, so I opted instead for 'Sinfield' which I'd seen on the wall of the gent's in a Covent Garden wine bar (get me, the man about town). Part of the reason for choosing it was I thought no one would ever get it wrong. Since then, I've been erroneously called everything from Sinclair to Singleton to - inevitably - Seinfeld (I wouldn't mind his cheques). Even when they do get the surname right, folk as often as not call me Pete. I once spent an entire article in *The Independent* being referred to as Pete Sinfield, who is actually a musician and songwriter, a former member of prog rock giants King Crimson who later confounded expectations by penning hits for Bucks Fizz. Happily though, when I was introduced to the lugubrious Scottish poet Ivor Cutler and he said…

IVOR: Your name is known to me.

…I immediately replied that he was probably thinking of Pete Sinfield but was pleasantly stunned to hear him respond…

IVOR: Oh no. I've never heard of him.

Anyway, I must have done something right at the audition (or they were short of male students) because I got in and soon began to familiarise myself with the college's cast of eccentrics. Our Head of Voice was an elderly dame called Eleanor whose vocal inflections reminded us of Kenny Everett. When not forcing us to negotiate tongue-twisters like 'Verily Valerie' or 'Ken Dodd's dad's dog's dead', she'd try to teach regional accents. Sadly, Eleanor's idea of Cockney was to say…

ELEANOR: Oi you, mush, come over 'ere.

…in a voice like that of Kenny Everett. This was followed by her version of Geordie, consisting of…

ELEANOR: Haway, the lads. Whan the boot cooms in.

…in a voice like that of Kenny Everett.

Years later, when *Eastenders* began, I pictured countless auditionees all saying…

AUDITIONEES: Oi you, mush…

…in a voice like that of Kenny Everett and being asked…

PRODUCER: Did you, by any chance, go to the Rose Bruford College?

For all her faults as a tutor, Eleanor was benign, whereas Gretl was fearsome and smoked not so much twenty a day as forty an hour (good idea for a voice coach). She it was who roundly berated one of my fellow students with the words…

GRETL: Mr. Oldman, until you have discarded your South London accent, you will never get anywhere as an actor.

As this Mr. Oldman's first name was Gary and as he retains his South London accent to this day (albeit tinged with Californian), I'm sure he'd love to go back and tell Gretl how wrong she was, but she's gone the way of Ken Dodd's dad's dog.

Gary Oldman had terrible trouble getting served in the pubs of Sidcup because at 18, he looked 16. Later, he did look 18, but by then he was 36. At least the landlord of The Ferret & Trouserleg only got Gary's age wrong. Our Classical Dance tutor went a step further. Theo Tucker was an octogenarian whose classes could have been scripted by Joyce Grenfell. Her catch-phrase is with me still:-

THEO: Thank you, Miss Lander, And...

whereupon the stern figure of Miss Lander, made-up to resemble Joan Crawford's scarier sister, would go from total inertia to pianistic dexterity as if Theo had been working her with a flick switch.

A child of the Victorian age, Theo didn't hold with these modern unisex changing facilities and insisted that...

THEO: All the gels should change at one end of the room and all the men should change at the other.

At one point, several weeks into this arrangement, she approached a fair-haired figure at the men's end and piped...

THEO: I thought I said all the gels should change at that end of the room.

GARY: What of it?

THEO: Run along then.

GARY: Eh? I'm not a gel.

[PAUSE]

THEO: Aren't you?

GARY: Nah.

THEO: I say, I'm most dreadfully sorry!

[EXIT THEO, TO BE REPLACED BY A MIDDLE-AGED WOMAN IN A BEIGE TROUSER SUIT WHO LOOKED LIKE PATRICK MOORE.]

Most of the time, Gary and I shared an ability to laugh at the excesses of luvviedom around us - and here I mean the staff as much as other students. Workshop sessions dissecting the pronouncements of Grotowski and his mate Stan E. Slavski had us in stitches almost as readily as lectures in Philosophy from a man who couldn't even pronounce the word. Well, in those pre-internet days we had to make our own entertainment. Our favourite philosophers were Pete and Dud - or, as they'd become, Derek and Clive.

I'd been lucky enough to catch their West End swan song at the Cambridge Theatre in a show called

Behind The Fridge where the stand-out sketch was a creepy little piece about a peer (Moore) being ferried to Westminster by Cook's psychotic mini-cab driver. It was by far the most mature chunk of writing in the show, if not their entire canon, but hardly anyone had heard of *The Mini-Drama*. Gary and I set out to rectify this (in Sidcup at least) by performing it as an extra-curricular lunchtime presentation with him as the peer and me as the driver - or rather, him as Moore and me as Cook since basically we did im-personations of them.

Fresh from a trip to the local breaker's yard, our enterprising stage manager Hiroshi Misago even rigged up a make-believe car on stage, complete with operational windscreen wipers (despite a notable lack of windscreen). I was very chuffed to read an interview Gary gave to Craig McLean for *The Daily Telegraph* weekend magazine nearly thirty years on in 2007 where he cited this as one of the best things he did at college. It was - but how good to know he thought so too.

Tragically, no record of it remains. We didn't have the resources (or the camera) to film it and the one audio cassette version disappeared when my (t)rusty Ford Anglia got nicked. I recovered the car...but in some ways the tape would have been worth more. Presumably, the miscreant had a listen, thought...

MISCREANT: (THINKING) Who are these wankers?

...and promptly binned it - or worse still, recorded *Wind and Wuthering* by Genesis over it. Home taping is killing theatre.

As our three-year sojourn in Sidcup's leafy purlieus drew to a close, Mr. O got himself a well-deserved contract with York Theatre Royal, setting in motion a phenomenal performing career...but I do wish he'd discard his South London accent.

I, on the other hand, was dithering. Full-time acting struck me as the ultimate oxymoron and I realised I needed another string to my bow. Actually, just getting a bow would have been a start. At first, I considered directing but a spell as assistant director on our final year production of Arthur Miller's laugh-a-minute knockabout farce *The Crucible* soon cured that.

As an assistant, you are required to carry out the director's instructions, no matter how crass you know them to be. Our man in charge was also the college Principal, someone calling himself Giovanni, though his real name was Norm, and he'd decided this *Crucible* was to be given a Brechtian interpretation. Just one problem: how do you bring a Brechtian interpretation to a script not written by Brecht? What would we do for an encore, *Run For Your Wife* as a Jacobean tragedy?

All I knew was that Muggins (should have been my stage name) got saddled with the joyous task of implementing dollops of Brecht at rehearsals on virtually a daily basis, Norm being otherwise engaged at a string of governors' meetings (lucky man). Howls of protests from the cast, all fellow third-year students, drew some feeble response from me along the lines of...

ME: (FEEBLY) I'm just follow-ing orders.

Doubtless, had I met Ken Livingstone at the time, he'd have accused me of being...

KEN: A Nazi concentration camp guard.

Unfairly, though: I wasn't that camp.

In the end, Norm was very kind to me, even treating me to a G. and T. in his office while complaining about the conditions on our mini-tour.

NORM: Do you know, Bob, when we stayed in Canterbury, the TV in my hotel room didn't even have a remote control!

ME: (ACTING MY LITTLE SOCKS OFF) Scandalous!

This was 1978 when most students were dead impressed by TVs that had a screen.

So, directing was out. True, I might have worked my way up to imposing Brechtian interpretations on *Starlight Express* but only after years of Nazi concentration camp guarding. What to do, then, to keep the wolf from hovering round my cat flap? The answer came to me when we staged a commedia dell'arte production, directed by Gary, where I was cast as Pantalone but also found myself functioning as a kind of script editor, collating the best of our improvised lines from rehearsals and turning them into a workable text. The mighty discipline of sitting at a typewriter (remember them?) and bashing out dialogue we could actually use on stage became addictive, especially as I was encouraged to embellish it with halfway decent gags of my own.

Good God, I thought, am I becoming the new Shakespeare? Or better still, the new Eddie Braben?

CLEVER WRITER: Did you know the playwright Aeschylus was killed by an eagle dropping a tortoise on his head?

STUPID WRITER: Hah! Everywhere you go: critics!

3

THE GREAT UNWATCHED

"As unemployment rose, it seemed the only people Thatcher kept in work were radio gag-writers."

I left drama school with that special something of which few actors can boast: an offer of work. Two hours helping out at a kids' workshop in Hammersmith on a Sunday afternoon might have been small beer but I never was a heavy drinker. They paid me £7.50 which was a lot of money in 1979 – well, it was if you were skint. The show at the Riverside Studios (three millimetres from my front door) was a platform for Patrick Barlow's alter ego, Professor Desmond Dingle, then a far more benign and bumbling character than the theatrical know-all he later became (Dingle that is, not Patrick). I was impressed by his ability to amuse and engage the junior punters without being patronising. He only talked down to them for practical reasons: they were smaller and he was standing up.

Having left college on the Friday and got a cash-in-hand, just-down-the-road gig two days later tempted me to think it would always be this easy. But I'd only got the Riverside job in the first place because one of my tutors, Robin Samson, happened to be involved and needed last-minute recruits. On the day, I must have created quite an impression as I never heard from him again. So, not knowing where the next £7.50 was coming from, I had to become pro-active – not an easy task as that particular slice of jargonese hadn't been invented yet. Happy days.

The BBC beckoned – but it didn't realise that at the time. I had to let it know it was beckoning. With that combination of cluelessness and arrogance that is the unique preserve of the 22-year-old, I rang Broadcasting

House and asked for a job. BH was out but its secretary told me there were no vacancies for unemployed ex-students. I pointed out that if they hired me, I wouldn't be unemployed, thereby solving the problem. Then something amazing happened: she didn't put the phone down.

Even more bizarrely, she arranged for me to see one of the Heads of Comedy. Comedy, as the cliché-peddlers are fond of reminding us, is a serious business. It's also a many-headed beast and, like the hydra, you can't remove one head without at least two growing in its place. The woman on the phone – later to become Janet Staplehurst, famed for blowing her whistle at sixty-second intervals on *Just A Minute* – fixed me up with one of comedy's smaller heads. I was to meet bigger ones later.

Malcolm Fraser was thick-set, tall, incredibly clumsy (he had once taken a live show off the air when a careless wave of his arm caused the needle to fly from the record it was playing to the nation) and looked more like a building society cashier than a comedy head. At the time, he was SELER (Script Editor, Light Entertainment, Radio) and while affable enough, betrayed no tendency towards humour of any kind – especially not the funny kind. He made it quite clear that Corporation staff jobs were only available to people who were not writer-performers. I'd have been in with a chance had I chosen to pursue a career in Personnel (or as it's now known, HRT) but creating scripts and acting in them was the preserve of the freelance. So I asked if he'd got any jobs for freelances but, displaying the lack of tendency for humour that I've already described, he didn't get that.

Instead, he pointed me towards two men with six names between them: Jonathan James-Moore and Griff Rhys Jones. They were the producers, respectively, of *The News Huddlines* and *Week Ending*, topical sketch shows whose list of writing credits could give the dead of two world wars a run for their money. They were the only radio programmes where the continuity announcer played the lead. Maybe that's why the jokes had to be short.

The News Huddlines was, as its name suggests, a vehicle for comedian Roy Hudd. I should explain that the term 'vehicle' in this context applies to a show that's transporting a particular artiste to their destination of, hopefully, the top of the ratings…though it could just as easily take a wrong turning, get stuck on the ring road, run out of gas and have to call the AA. I know it's not a perfect metaphor but give me a break, I didn't invent it. This kind of terminology is favoured by those Heads of Comedy who often fail to recognise its absurdity. One particularly dour gag writer, the ironically-named Eric Merriman, was once asked to think of a vehicle for Ernie Wise. He suggested a hearse.

Anyway, *The News Huddlines* was still a vehicle for Roy Hudd. Back in the day, it was always helpful if a star's name could be incorporated punningly into the show's title. David Jason was given a series called *The Jason Explanation* because his surname <u>nearly</u> rhymed with 'explanation'. Well, I didn't say it was foolproof. The worst one, though, reared its head when Alfred Marks, having appeared on telly in *Alfred Marks Time* (not bad), ended his days in the Radio Two 'vehicle' *Marks In His Diary* (oh dear, sounds a bit grubby, like the town councillor who wanted to put Staines on the map).

Anyway, *The News Huddlines* remained a vehicle for Roy Hudd. Well, it was a long series. Started by producer John Lloyd in the mid-'70s, it ran for over twenty-five years and only came to an end due to Roy's *Coronation Street* commitments. He had to stay in and watch it three nights a week. Good God, hadn't the man heard of videos?

Previously, I'd not been a Hudd fan – but then I'd only ever seen him on TV. Roy had a peak-time sketch series in the late '60s called *The Illustrated Weekly Hudd*. Don't bother looking for the pun this time - it isn't there. One of showbiz's premier wordsmiths, Dick Vosburgh, had suggested calling it 'RH Positive' but perhaps BBC1 thought the public were so thick they'd think it was a show about blood groups. Pity. Ardal O'Hanlon could have starred in the sequel 'O Negative', best viewed on a plasma screen.

The main problem with Roy Hudd on telly was that he never seemed to know which to play to, the camera or the studio audience. For the viewer at home, few things are more disconcerting than a performer who's ignoring you in favour of the unseen punters. Besides, Roy was unlucky in that the camera 'wasn't kind to him'. This was pointed out to me later by a man called Bob Davis who became a household name in the mid '70s (trust me) but on radio, none of that mattered. Mr Hudd was a giant of a stand-up comic and when I saw him 'work the room' at a *Huddlines* recording, all thoughts of his TV awkwardness were erased from my mind (though not entirely or there'd be a gap where much of this paragraph sits).

The News Huddlines format – largely unchanged across twenty-five years – consisted of an opening monologue, several lengthy sketches (that's five minutes top weight to you and me), a couple of song parodies and about a week and a half of writers' credits.

YOU: Why so many writers for such a brief stroll down comedy lane?

...I pretend to hear you ask. The answer lies, not in the soil as Kenneth Williams used to say on *Beyond Our Ken*, but in that opening monologue. At one o'clock on a recording day, Roy would bound onto the stage of the Paris Theatre (so-called because it was in London), clutching half-a-dozen sheets of freshly-typed A4. This material was all based on stuff out of that morning's papers (you remember papers: they were what passed for news before Wikileaks came along) and the star of the show had barely had time to skim them, having spent three hours rehearsing the rest of the programme. Okay, he didn't have to learn it – one of the great attractions of radio, along with the staggering fees – but it's a considerable craft to perform audience comedy on-mike while working off a script…and I've never seen anyone do it better.

In the cast at that time were the gifted and underrated Chris Emmett (who stayed till the 21st century) and Janet Brown who left in the early '80s when she became to Margaret Thatcher what Mike Yarwood had been to Harold Wilson. Maggie – or Hurricane Hilda as she was none-too-affectionately known – had seized power in the early summer of '79 and, as unemployment rose, it seemed the only people she kept in work were radio gag-writers. In her impersonation, Janet Brown was reluctant to go for the jugular in quite the way Steve Nallon did a few years later on *Spitting Image*. Perhaps she sensed the carrot of an OBE being dangled if she could just keep it nice and uncontroversial. Thankfully, the men putting words in her mouth had other ideas. They <u>were</u> all men then: it was a real testosterzone. Star creative forces like Janey Preger and Debbie Barham would come later. Deb was at most a year old at the time, probably penning jokes of genius in her cot. Most of the late '70s *Huddlines* sketches were the work of Laurie Rowley, Terry Ravenscroft and Andy Hamilton – and it was Andy's sharp satirical stabs at our glorious leader that met with Janet's disapproval. Happily though, Andy was very persistent and common sense - and comedy – prevailed. So it was that Radio Two's audience were treated to an Iron Lady soundalike saying she was all in favour of short sentences…like "fetch a rope" and "shoot the lot".

After La Brown came Alison Steadman for a while and eventually June Whitfield whose PM incarnation was easily as good as Janet's and who later recreated her *Take It From Here* character Eth whenever the script called for Norma Major. By then, I was long gone from the smoke-filled writers' room (so-called because it was crammed with smoke-filled writers).

Huddlines was a tricky show to perfect, requiring as it did the ability to get a big laugh out of every news item. As our blunt Yorkshire script editor Laurie Rowley put it…

LAURIE: What I want is thigh-slappers.

…and too often, Laurie's thighs remained unslapped by me.

I was having more luck with *Week Ending*, possibly because the script didn't need to be quite so funny. With no studio audience to amuse and no Yorkshire thighs to slap, you could concentrate on the satire and the business of getting your point across. If that sounds like the recipe for a ten-course banquet of self-indulgence, well, occasionally it was – but by the time I stumbled into Griff Rhys Jones's barely-carpeted office, he'd been producing the show for a couple of years and was highly adept at filtering the crap. He was also proficient in training raw recruits, of which I was the newest - and the rawest. No one can teach you to write comedy but, if some spark of talent is there, a decent producer should be able to spot and nurture it. It was thanks to Griff that in no time I was earning the basic rate of £8.25 per minute of material used plus £5 for a 'quickie' (the latter being a catch-all, smutty-sounding term for a one-liner or sketch under thirty seconds). The best way to 'up your rates' was always to write in as many sound effects (F/X) as possible, thereby pushing the sketch into the next chargeable minute without having to think up any additional dialogue - not that I ever did anything like that, of course.

F/X: BIG   BEN   STRIKES
MIDNIGHT; GALLANT SIX-HUNDRED
RIDE INTO VALLEY OF DEATH;
HELL FREEZES OVER.

Some of my fellow writers were hilarious…unintentionally. One cove with falsetto tones and a beach-ball beer-belly would storm in, snatch up the office phone and call British Rail (at the expense of you, the licence-payer) to complain about the dirty train he'd travelled up on from Canterbury, his opening line being…

COVE: Get me Sir Peter Parker!

…who was then chairman of the company - and of course <u>he's</u> going to get the Marigolds on instanta, isn't he? Another of the typewriter-batterers among us was obsessed with learning 'the secret of comedy', as if such a thing existed. Actually, it does exist but I can't tell you what it is: it's a secret.

But back to the producer presiding over this gaggle of goons (i.e. us). The Griff of the late '70s was very different from the Griff of today: back then, he was a lot older. Clad head-to-toe in herring-bone tweed (with, no doubt, tweed y-fronts underneath), he reminded me of a middle-aged GP whereas he was, in fact, a middle-aged GP's son. So was I – but other than that, we weren't related. Anybody who's met Griff since about 1982 would never have him down as a drinker. That's because he used up his lifetime's quota of alcohol in the '70s. The Horse & Groom in Great Portland Street and a now-defunct out-of-hours drinking club called The Marie Lloyd took it in turns playing host to Griff and his fellow ex-Cambridge Footlights stars Rory McGrath and his mate Ashley. I'd last seen Rory on our final day at Redruth Grammar School in 1974 and since leaving altar-boyhood behind, he was a changed man, now cutting a porky, bearded figure with a bottomless capacity for alcohol and a form of blood sport called Griff-baiting. The victim of this (Griff of course, do keep up) seemed to enjoy it in a curious way, despite the fact that it was often unsubtle to the point of savagery. Perhaps anything's better than being ignored.

Ashley and Rory were writing a

lot of radio comedy shows for old-school turns like Don McLean, Windsor Davies and Frankie Howerd who took a shine to them in the showers (less of that later). Well, officially that's what they were doing, though they put far more energy into rewriting their deadlines and slagging off other shows. They were particularly scathing about *The Hitch-Hiker's Guide To The Galaxy* and its creator, Douglas Adams (though not, of course, because he was considerably more successful than the pair of them).

Neither had much time for *Week Ending*, come to that, especially Ashley. This was unfortunate for us as in 1980, he took over as producer and was, frankly, about as much use as a cellophane crash-helmet. Apart from addressing cast and writers alike with thinly-veiled contempt (which at least proves he was an egalitarian), he was always in such a hurry to get away after the recording that one week he left the studio without bothering to take the programme tape. That building is now part of a health club, so if you're a fitness fanatic in the Lower Regent Street area and in mid-squat thrust you stumble upon a ten-inch spool of metal oxide, it could well be the show that time (and the producer) forgot..

After what seemed like an eternity for us as well as him, Ashley strutted off in his white loafers to be a multi-millionaire in TV, leaving us to the far more tender mercies of the splendidly dippy Paul Mayhew-Archer. Following this nuclear winter for the programme, once more we had a producer who actually gave a toss about it! Paul and I got on because I did too: I'd been a fan for years.

Launched in 1970, *Week Ending* was radio's somewhat tardy response to *TW3*, a weekly sketch-based pop at the establishment. There had been other attempts at this format including *Better Late* starring stage revue veteran Peter Reeves and the now-forgotten *Listen To This Space* with Nicholas Parsons (well, forgotten by all except Nicholas Parsons) but these were short-lived while *Week Ending* enjoyed a run of nearly thirty years, man and boy. Such programmes tend to divide the audience into two camps: those who think the BBC's a bunch of Commie bastards for allowing this subversive filth onto the air and those who think the BBC's a bunch of lily-livered wankers for not letting it go far enough. 'Friday Night with the Soggy Liberals' was suggested as an alternative title by one of the latter type of dissenters. Sadly, he was among my fellow writers so if that was his opinion, Christ knows what the punters must have thought.

There was certainly enough disapproval pouring forth from the Green Ink Brigade, that section of the listenership with a mission to complain. I was once told by one of their representatives that I would...

GREEN INKER: ...do well on Channel Four!

(not, I suspect, intended as a compliment). I wrote back, thanking my well-wisher for his kind prediction of a lucrative career for me in commercial telly. I'd earned this rebuke by tackling a 'Queen Mum gets fishbone stuck in throat' incident as it might have been commemorated by the then Poet Laureate, Sir John Betjeman. I forget most of it – probably just as well – but I'm sure there was a couplet along the lines of…

BETJEMAN: With the pudding still to follow,

You found your haddock hard to swallow.

Still, it all ended happily with the offending item safely removed, leaving the old dear with nothing in her mouth except a plum. Hardly the stuff to bring down the monarchy but you'd be amazed how sensitive royalists are on their idols' behalf. Or maybe you wouldn't. Perhaps it was you who wrote to me…or might you, I wonder, have penned a note to one of my colleagues after he knocked out this item:-

NEWSREADER: Princess Margaret

threw a party to celebrate her half-century. Roddy was there but the other 49 couldn't make it.

Even if you're too young to know who these people were, the whole thing's pretty self-explanatory. On hearing it, one listener suggested that...

LISTENER: The author should be taken to Trafalgar Square and publicly horse-whipped!

As the 'author' in question was a devotee of hard-core pornography, this might have proved to be more pleasure than punishment.

Important stories got us into trouble too. When a British nurse called Helen Smith fell from a balcony at an illegal drinks party in Saudi Arabia, I wrote a piece attacking our Foreign Office for its puny efforts to investigate the highly suspicious circumstances of her death. A close relative of Helen's (possibly her sister) complained to the BBC that such a tragedy should not be the basis of a comedy sketch. Clearly it was a sensitive issue for the bereaved but this kind of argument misses the point.

True, there are those who think all humour should be mere froth whereas I believe shows like *Week Ending* are at their best when using wit as a weapon. Call me a pompous old fart if you like. I can't hear you: this is a book.

David Hatch, the HLER (Head of Light Entertainment, Radio) stood by me on that one and I was grateful to him. He fought the programme's corner at the inevitable board meeting when the matter got referred upwards to a man called MDR. Well, that's what HLER called him but his real name was Aubrey Singer (Managing Director, Radio). As I write this, Singer's obituaries dominate what used to be called the broadsheets but they've all omitted my favourite story about him, told to me by one of that canny breed, the studio managers (the grown-ups who actually know how to work the equipment). When Margaret

Thatcher visited Broadcasting House (presumably stock-taking prior to her proposed privatisation), Aubrey Singer proudly showed her round a drama studio, then proffered...

SINGER: Now Prime Minister, if you'd care to accompany me up here...

...and promptly led her up a sound effects staircase that didn't go anywhere. On reaching the top and realising this, he segued into...

SINGER: And now, if you'd care to accompany me back down again...

Local radio is often a source of this kind of unintentional hilarity, usually at the expense of the station's top brass. Many 'suits' have little understanding of - and even less interest in - what goes into something called a 'programme'. One extreme example occurred in 1984 when I was working as a presenter for Guildford's County Sound. They decided to keep in touch with the public by inviting coach parties to tour the building, Longleat-style. So the MD was shepherding a gaggle of pensioners round the premises one evening when he blundered into the record library, an area he appeared to know absolutely nothing about. Sitting among the LPs, preparing that night's show, I actually heard him say...

```
MD: Ah yes, now this is the
um...record library.   Yes.
Not an especially big record
library.   I mean, the BBC up
in London for instance has a
far larger...er...record lib-
rary.   Yes.
```

There was then a good deal of reverse shuffling as MD and OAPs returned to the relative safety of the corridor, where the MD's voice boomed enthusiastically...

```
MD: Now,  this  is  a  vital
piece  of  equipment  in  any
radio   station:   the   notice
board!
```

Three people fainted with excitement.

*

Back at *Week Ending*, Hatch of the BBC (as HLER had been known in his performing life on *I'm Sorry, I'll Read That Again*) had started *Week Ending* himself in 1970, along with Simon Brett, and was on record as saying he felt the show would never truly fulfil its brief till somebody sued it. When someone finally did, he went fucking mental.

A man whom we'll call Derek Jarman who had been far more graphically – and a lot less subtly – pilloried in *Private Eye*, took exception to a monologue written about him by John Langdon, subsequently one of Rory Bremner's most dependable creatives (in all aspects save his time-keeping). John was taking the same kind of line as the *Eye* on Jarman's character and ability as a tabloid editor. While they dubbed him 'Sid Yobbo', Langdon went wittier and described him as 'the man who thinks that erudite is a glue'.

Early on, it must have been made clear to Jarman by someone vaguely connected with the law that there was nothing to be gained by taking Auntie to court over one sketch heard by a few thousand soggy liberals over cocoa between *A Book at Bedtime* and the shipping forecast.   Accordingly, the prosecution raised its game by accusing us of mounting a systematic campaign of character assassination against the plaintiff. Two things here:-

1)   The idea that a bunch of scruffy herberts in ill-fitting jeans and tank tops could mount a systematic piss-up in The Horse and Groom stretched credibility to breaking point.

2)   Even if we had been capable of such a thing, we'd doubtless have gone for bigger fish. Jarman was virtually unknown to the vast majority of the British public (sadly, a state of affairs that wasn't to last much longer).

Still, that was their case – and so it was that complete episodes of *Week Ending* (though probably not the one Ashley had left behind) had to be loaded onto a tape recorder and played in the Strand: a West End gig at last. The Judge sided with numerous radio critics by telling the court this was not a laughing matter. Good job it wasn't the *Huddlines* or there might have been an outbreak of thigh-slapping in the jury box.

The opposition must have known they were in trouble because Delboy turned up in a sober blue pin-stripe number with pince-nez specs, presumably to make himself look more erudite. In desperation, his counsel cross-examined one of the programme's producers, Alan Nixon. Unused to wearing a suit and having only recently grown a beard to hide his skin complaint, Alan looked decidedly shifty and kept his hand over his mouth while answering the hostile questions. The prosecutor pounced, declaiming,

PROSECUTOR: Do speak up, Mr Nixon. I'm sure the jury would love to hear what you have to tell us.

This guy had been reading too much *Rumpole*. Such cheap tricks aside, things weren't going well for Del. His team had failed to establish that a string of sketches written by the marvellously prolific Guy Jenkin were directed at him. The anonymous red-top editor portrayed by Bill Wallis in them bore a Glaswegian brogue wholly un-reminiscent of Jarman's poshed-up sergeant-major cockney. Also, the only real thigh-slapper of the case came when the defence produced proof of John's argument that DJ had introduced nakedness to *The Daily Express* (as encapsulated in the line, "All the nudes fit to print and all the news printed to fit"). A photo from the snot-rag concerned was held up in court, revealing a topless model. Derek refuted the nudity claim with the words…

JARMAN: She's wearing a hat!

Wish I was erudite like him.

He lost. Boy, how he lost. £70,000 was the grand total he was ordered to pay, though I have it on good authority that the BBC never pressed him for it. Instead, the bloody fools gave him the Radio Two breakfast show! Such a good idea, I'm sure you'll agree, to follow seasoned professionals like Terry Wogan, Ken Bruce and the stunningly witty Ray Moore with someone who sounded like he'd never anchored a radio programme in his life. So ask yourself this, dear licence-payer, who was the real loser?

Hilariously, I was approached by a producer called Graham Pass to present a weekly slot on said breakfast programme, spotlighting some of the great names of radio comedy. Tactfully, I omitted John Langdon from the list but I did wonder whether any cheery banter with the Beeb's new golden boy might be slightly soured by my association with *Week Ending* (tainted with criminality, I believe the expression is). No such bad luck: Del was far too full of his own importance to care about anyone else and once a week we greeted each other civilly across the desk. I say 'desk' but he couldn't operate the knobs as radio presenters are supposed to. He didn't even understand the term for it:

self-drive. He thought this meant the BBC wouldn't send a car for him.

Various stand-ins were found for Derek whenever he went on holiday. Occasionally, we'd actually get a professional broadcaster like Bob Holness (in fact, very like him) but mostly it was Jarman's Fleet Street cronies such as Nina Myskow, Jean Rook and someone I'd already worked with in a voiceover capacity on BBC1's *Points of View*. In her radio days, this woman (whom we'll call Ann Tagonistic) would refer on-air to the studio engineers as…

ANN: Monkeys behind the glass.

…till the day came when one of them took revenge by fading her out in mid-flow, then whispering into her headphones…

ENGINEER: The monkeys are getting restless.

It was the headphones that provided one 'monkey' with the best comeback of all. On entering the studio one morning, Annie dearest was appalled to see her 'cans' lying unplugged on her desk. Indignantly, she turned to the duty engineer and spat...

ANN: Do I have to plug these in myself?!

ENGINEER: Can if you like, Ann, but you're meant to plug them in the desk.

Collapse of stunted ginger party.

But further high Jarman jinks weren't far off. When his programme attracted a number of complaints from listeners, Derek's sidekick, Vivien Stuart, took the show's executive producer to task on-air in her capacity as presenter of the radio equivalent of *Points of View*. Delboy, incensed at what he saw as her betrayal, left an abusive message on Vivien's answer-phone, describing her as a...

JARMAN:...toffee-nosed cow!

With a command of language like that, you can see how he conquered the tabloids. Somehow – Lord knows how – this message was copied, looped and used as a kind of rap over a single by

The Wonder Stuff called *The Size of a Cow*, then played on my friend Adrian Juste's Saturday lunchtime Radio One show. Consternation broke out in the BBC when the red tops seized on this risible example of Auntie using her left hand to shoot herself in the right foot and a post mortem of epic proportions began. How had this happened? Who was responsible? Tragically, that will never be revealed. I mean, there was only one link between the Jarman show and Adrian, and if <u>he</u> doesn't know the miscreant's identity, well...

After the court case (remember that?), one *Week Ending* stalwart – a Scouser named Barry Bowes – summed up the state of affairs by saying...

BARRY: The show was meant to be writ with wit...but now the wit comes first and the writ follows.

Suddenly, producers became very sensitive lest our season in the Strand got a re-run. I remember the occasional visitation from departmental big-wigs like SELER (that's right, Malcolm Fraser) and AHLER (Edward 'Ted' Taylor). You've probably sussed that Ted was the Assistant Head, Light Entertainment, Radio. Shame he wasn't the Managing Assistant Head, then we could have called him Gustav. One for the Radio Three fans there.

These cameo appearances were much along the lines of the Gus 'I'm not here' figure in *Drop The Dead Donkey*, written, coincidentally I'm sure, by Andy Hamilton and Guy Jenkin, both *Week Ending* veterans (and subsequently the authors and directors of *Outnumbered*). Andy was very adept at sliding characters from the BBC Langham Street building into his works of fiction. There was a commissionaire called Des at the Beeb who became a commissionaire called Des in the ITV series, *Shelley*. Des was fond of demonstrating his distinctive brand of humour to the comedy folk not bothering to flash their passes at him, especially the ones carrying instruments. *Radio Active* writer/star Philip Pope couldn't arrive bearing a guitar case without Des offering this gem…

DES: Been busking then? Eh? I say, you been busking then, eh? Eh? Busking?

Phil's acting talent was stretched beyond reason as he pretended never to have heard this before. The hilarity subsided, though, whenever an IRA bomb scare mobilised the Corporation security guards into protective action. Suddenly, it was all…

DES: May I see your pass, sir?

One of our number, Matthew Vosburgh (son of Dick) turned up passless on such a day and Des refused to admit him on the grounds that he might be a terrorist he'd never seen before…despite having seen him every day for the past six months. All he could do, he said, was ring the producer concerned and ask if he recognised Matthew's name. Revenge came as Dick's lad gave his full name as 'Matthew Jobsworth Vosburgh' and Des wrote it down soberly, then called the office to tell them a Mr Jobsworth Vosburgh was in reception. To this day, he's probably wondering why they laughed. Must have been the way he told it.

Week Ending – yes, we're still on that – very nearly qualified as a regular job. Running for forty weeks of each year, it was almost as much a fixture of Radio Four as the farming report and the use of the word 'empowerment' on *Woman's Hour*. Perhaps that's why the *Radio Times* commissioned an article on us by humour heavyweight Barry Took and sent a photographer to one of our writers' meetings. Having been tipped off that a camera would be in the room, a young bearded Oxford graduate called Angus Deayton turned up in a three-piece suit and sat incongruously among the rest of us, all attired like tramps as usual. Sadly for this ambitious youth, the published photograph was so poorly lit that all the reader saw was a distant image of Ashley (still in command then) at the head of the dusty table, surrounded by blurry blobs in indistinguishable clothing. I don't think Angus came again. Took's article caused dissent in the *News Huddlines* camp due to a perceived slight against its writers. They exacted revenge by giving Roy Hudd a line about Barry Took that went…

ROY: I remember him when he was Marty Feldman's typist.

…but the producer cut it out, so you've just witnessed its world premiere.

Angus, meanwhile, took off his suit and devoted himself to a series called *Radio Active* which ran for years and featured characters with names like Anna Daptor, Mike Flex, Mike Channel and, controversially, Mike Hunt. In fact, this only became controversial after about three series when Malcolm Fraser (SELER) came storming down the corridor and berated the producer Jamie Rix (son of Brian) for daring to allow such a name into the script. When Jamie pointed out that Mike Hunt had featured in all three previous series, SELER huffed and puffed for a bit before screaming...

SELER: Well, take him out!

That's executive decision-making for you. I was once told by one of SELER's colleagues that the departmental script editor's job was to take out all the offensive words the writers put in, like 'bloody'...on the grounds that such a term could upset women at a particular time of the month!

Getting back to *Week Ending* - again -it really was the nearest thing this country had to a radio comedy writing school. The register of those who went on to bigger and better (and in some cases, smaller and worse) things includes Alistair Beaton, Peter Spence, David Renwick, Nick Revell, James Hendrie, Arnold Brown, Pete Sinclair, Dave Cohen, Debbie Barham, Steve Punt, John O'Farrell, Jeremy Hardy, Angus Deayton, his suit...ah, the list is endless. Oh, it's ended. Renwick, creator of

Victor Meldrew, later wrote an article for *The Guardian* recalling the moment he realised that beautifully-crafted sketches crammed with political allusions were no match in comic value for David Jason standing on a chair, making seagull noises. His point was that, in broadcast comedy, you are only as funny as your performers.

I agree. Of the cast I worked with, Jason was by far the least intellectual and politically aware but easily the most maverick, unpredictable and fun to write for. In his hands, I heard many an indifferent piece of material (sometimes my own) become transformed into a dazzling display of comedic acrobatics. Something puzzled me, though: I was never sure why he insisted on wearing a cap in the studio for months on end till the day he removed it to reveal a far more plentiful head of hair than he'd had before putting it on.

Some now famous acting names breezed through our portals en route to

the high life. Actually, a few of them –
like Tim Brooke-Taylor, Martin Jarvis
and Miriam Margolyes - had lives that
were pretty high already, but a diffident
young chap called Jonathan Pryce made
quite an impression (we knew he had the
makings of a Bond villain the moment
we spotted that cat on his lap) as did Bill
Nighy whom I recall playing a door-to-
door salesman of crap goods purveyed
by a dodgy Soviet outfit, Gorky
Industries. In James Hendrie's take on
this improbable-but-true story, the
peddler offers various useless products
to an increasingly bored housewife
(played by a genuinely bored Elsie
Flashtea). Eventually, she tries to get rid
of him but, salesman to the last, he jams
his foot in the door. Unhappily for him,
his shoes are Gorky Industries standard
issue, so the next thing we hear is the
snap of cheap plastic followed by Bill
swearing in fluent Russian. As we know,
he went on to turn hesitation into an art
form, which could be why they've never
had him on *Just A Minute*.

The other regular troupers around

this time were grumpy and gruff Bill Wallis who could pull a performance of great sensitivity out of the hat...when he could be bothered; David Tate, a versatile actor who did so many lucrative voiceovers that his Friday mornings with us could almost be classed as voluntary work; and as mentioned earlier, Elsie Flashtea whom I first saw in *The Frost Report.* She then worked on *The Illustrated Weekly Hudd* and Kenneth Horne's ITV outing *Horne-A-Plenty* but by the time she came to do *Week Ending*, was frankly a bit jaded. Some weeks, nothing seemed to please her. She hated it if there wasn't enough for her to do so the next week we'd ply her with material. That didn't go down well either as she liked to make an early getaway. One Friday, after producer Jan Ravens (yes, her out of *Dead Ringers*) had moved things round considerably and considerately in an effort to release Elsie as early as possible, Ms Flashtea's parting words were...

ELSIE: About bloody time!

...and we never saw her again. Well, not on that show anyway. As an actor, I worked with Elsie on a pilot show twenty-five years later and we got on fine. About bloody time too.

For a spell, Alison Steadman filled the gap as she had done when Janet Brown left the *Huddlines* (at the time, Alison was pregnant and loved doing radio because one's shape is kind of immaterial) and then a new resident actress joined the team. Tracey Ullman was very young (well, compared to the rest) and had no previous experience in radio – but she did have her own TV series...or a third of it. By this time, my colleague Tony Sarchet (fond of twiddling his hair round his finger) and I were the principal writers on *Week Ending* and Tracey liked our stuff enough to get us a gig on this new fangled medium called television. It'll never catch on with a name like that.

Q: Why do writers never say anything twice?

A: There's nothing in the contract about repeat fees.

4

THE RULE OF THREE

"Tracey Ullman hated jokes. A slight drawback on a comedy show?"

Telly folk - they're a panic, aren't they? Always rushing hither and thither, sometimes both at once, the only way they avoid coronaries is by not staying still long enough to have one.

There used to be a man called Russell Harty with a camp, school-masterly manner. In fact, I think he had been a teacher prior to becoming the Parky-lite of the TV chat shows.

For his 1981 Christmas special, it was decided that all the guests would do something they didn't normally do. Patrick Moore would play the xylophone; comic character actor Deryck Guyler would don thimbles and attack the washboard. The small detail that they'd been seen doing these same routines on countless shows since Logie

Baird's eureka moment was conveniently overlooked.

I was there to provide a Margaret Thatcher monologue for Maureen Lipman whose skill at apeing the fearsome old bat genuinely was a well-kept secret. In reality, Maureen and her husband Jack Rosenthal were both staunch Socialists (who lived in a big house in Hampstead) and here was a chance for her to portray the PM in her full horror to a mainstream audience at peak time - and hopefully get a few laughs.

Clad in her blonde wig and blue shoulder-pads, Maureen caused a certain amount of bafflement backstage. The veteran comic Sandy (Can You Hear Me, Mother?) Powell, looking at least 106 by then, shook her hand warmly, declaring that he'd always wanted to meet her. A party of cross-party MPs who'd been booked to sing carols with Anita Harris were less confused and roared approvingly at the prospect of their PM being savagely sent up by the star of the sitcom *Agony*.

All except one. After the rehearsal for that night's live transmission, Maureen and I were approached by the harrassed figure of producer Tom Gutteridge who revealed…

TOM: We've had a complaint from David Steele.

Baffled, we countered that there wasn't anything in it that even mentioned David Steele.

TOM: I know. That's the complaint.

Rather in the manner of what subsequently happened on *Spitting Image*, the party leader was livid at being ignored and insisted on some sort of barb against him. Anything's better than being forgotten - especially for a Liberal.

As chief wit, scribe and keeper of all things comedic, I put my brain into gear immediately…and couldn't think of anything. Thankfully though, Maureen could and she inserted a reference to David and his SDP confederate Shirley Williams, describing them as…

MAUREEN [IN HER THATCHER VOICE]: Sapphire and Steele.

It was a series of the time starring Joanna Lumley and David McCallum. Much to our delight - and presumably, David Steele's - this line went a storm…and the rest of the skit proved popular too. Sandy Powell's deliberately bad ventriloquist act was one of the funniest things I've ever seen and I'm so glad to have witnessed it live.

But possibly the strangest sight of all, that Yuletide, was that of *Tomorrow's World* and Farnborough Air Day stalwart Raymond Baxter in 1920s drag, wig and make-up, singing *I Went To A Marvellous Party*. Now, that really <u>was</u> unexpected.

All of the above took place in a building called The Greenwood Theatre, round the back of Guy's Hospital.

YOU: So what was a theatre doing there?

…I'm sure I heard you ask. Well, it seems a wealthy gentleman named

Greenwood had made provision in his will for 'an operating theatre' but somewhere in the maze of legal paperwork, this phrase got twisted and emerged as 'an operational theatre'. I don't suppose it saved as many lives as Mr. Greenwood had intended but, in later years when BBC1's *Question Time* was transmitted from there, it must have been ideal for sedation.

Elsewhere in this televisual kingdom of hustle twinned with bustle, one tiny figure towered above the socks of the rest. He was fast and often furious. He was K. Paul Jackson (or Kev to his friends), a man with killer ants in his pants.

The first thing that struck me about Kev, on entering his miniscule office in 1982, was that he held the world speed talking record. Just imagine an old 45 revolutions-per-minute gramophone record being played at 78. I don't need to: I've met Kev. Having been more accustomed to the leisurely delivery and pace of the average radio producer (and many of them <u>were</u> average), I had to learn Jacksonese fast…because that's how it was spoken.   Tony Sarchet, a lugubrious figure reminiscent of Jack Dee (but for the fact that Jack didn't exist yet) sat beside me, twiddling his hair as was his wont and, like me, struggling to take in Kev's every word while Tracey Ullman behaved as if nothing extraordinary was happening. Perhaps she was used to him by then.

Three of a Kind was a 1980s BBC sketch show, not to be confused with a 1960s BBC sketch show called *Three of a Kind*. This wouldn't be my last stint on a programme with a second-hand title.   Originally, the '80s incarnation was to have been named *Six of a Kind* but this ingenious plan came to grief when four of them got fired.   The survivors were a young man called Lenny Henry and an unyoung man called David Copperfield.   Not the magician who walked through walls so much as a comedian who sometimes walked into them. Tracey became the third man after being spotted playing a blinder in a Les Blair play at the Royal Court Theatre and her straight acting experience was to have a profound effect on the material we wrote for her...and when I say 'we', I mean the entire writing team: 300 of a kind.

She hated jokes. A slight drawback on a comedy show? So what we had to do was start with a strong character, then slip the gags in so obliquely that she barely noticed their presence. Early on, I gave her a monologue titled 'Roz' which involved her sitting in the lotus position on a beanbag and addressing the viewer directly in hip, upmarket tones, thus:-

ROZ: Hi. My name's Roz right? And, like, you know, I live in this basement bedsit in Cla'am yah, which has reeeeally helped me to see things at street level. I mean God, the people here are so <u>real</u>! So like I've decided to take up social work, yah? Okay so I don't have the qualifications:

for a start, I've never been an unmarried mother - I was going to be but I found out it involved having kids uuurgghh!

While I'd based Roz on someone I'd endured at drama school, Tracey modelled her performance on someone she'd endured at stage school. But the source of my endurance had gone on to full-time obscurity while Tracey's had become a famous face on *Top of the Pops*. Of course, I was never required to go on TV chat shows and talk about these things, but Tracey was - and on an edition of Tim Rice's programme, she revealed to him and around six million others that she'd based her portrayal on a Pan's People dancer called Rosemary. As the number of dancers called Rosemary in Pan's People totalled a maximum of one, it came as no surprise that the Rosemary in question (and everyone who knew her) realised this somewhat unflattering caricature was meant to be her. The next time their paths crossed, possibly on *Top of the Pops* as Tracey also enjoyed huge chart success, Rosemary described this treachery as...

ROSEMARY: ...<u>so</u> uncool.

Just what Roz would have said.

Mind you, she did have a point. Alan Plater, one of the best writers ever to enliven the radio and TV schedules, once said he didn't like people to recognise themselves in his work as he felt that was a form of betrayal. Besides, fictional characters are often a hybrid of several people. I make this point for the benefit of the *Big Brother* generation who might never have seen a work of TV fiction, apart from those programmes describing themselves as documentaries.

I forget who created David Copperfield's Medallion Man but it was rumoured to have been based on a BBC Radio One disc-jockey (or possibly on all of them). Apart from medallion-wearing, this figure's main function in life was the tireless and, as it turned out, futile pursuit of women, all of them of course played by Tracey. For two such diverse individuals, David and Tracey worked superbly well together if the material was right. Their parody of a plastic pop duo called Dollar was a comic high point, thanks to a storming lyric by Kim Fuller (brother of Simon Fuller, the sixth Spice Girl). These new words were put to the tune of *Give Me Back My Heart* which, as I'm sure you know, reached the all-important number four spot in the UK chart.

What you might <u>not</u> know, unless you're a showbiz lawyer, is that we fun factory labourers can't just plonk our own words on top of an existing melody without the composer's permission. The customary solution to this is for a new tune to be knocked up which bears a striking resemblance to the original, but not so striking as to end up being reprised in the High Court. After all the larks the judiciary had had with Derek Jarman, we didn't want to spoil them with musical entertainment as well. In this instance, however, no such sound-alike number was concocted for some reason, so Kim found himself in the slightly improbable and hugely unenviable position of having to perform his jottings down the phone to Dollar's songwriters. To everyone's amazement, they loved it and told Kim he clearly had the same opinion of the singers as they did.

The end result was delivered with pinpoint accuracy by our counterfeit Dollar (or Dollop as they were known) but as the series wore on, David Copperfield began to feel increasingly marginalised. It was turning into 'Two Of A Kind Plus David' where once it had been 'Two Of A Kind Plus Tracey', because Lenny Henry was becoming ever more influenced by Tracey's 'proper acting' approach to the sketches. Prior to working with her, his performances in the likes of *Tiswas* consisted largely of goofing about. High quality goofing about, I grant you, but goofing about none the less. Once he began working with someone who believed in believability, Lenny's conversion to this new faith was there for us all to see and rejoice in. Well, nearly all: it left Coppers out on a limb, not just because he was the least skilful actor of the trio but because his philosophy was determinedly old-fashioned. David's aim was to become the new Benny Hill but in that decade of political correctness and 'alternative' comedy, even the old Benny Hill was struggling to get work. In the light of this, David tended towards defensiveness, even belligerence and his performance on-camera suffered. He didn't always learn his lines properly and at times you can see him looking at the autocue instead of at Lenny or Tracey. Clever editing by the ever-cheerful Mykola Pavluk and high-speed Kev invariably rescued his transgressions from the comedy abyss.

That said, there were still times, even in the third and final series, when they all worked well together, as if on the same wavelength The 'top and tail' of the programme changed radically at that point. In series one and two, each edition opened and closed with the cast addressing the viewer directly with a string of snappy three-liners. David would tell us he had sex once a week and was quite happy. Tracey would say she had sex twice a week and was very happy. Lenny would declare he had sex once a year and was bloody delirious: it was tonight.

As you'll have guessed, Tracey found these vignettes about as much fun as minefield disco-dancing. After twelve such grisly experiences (or twenty-four if you count the tails as well as the tops), she'd had enough and in order to stave off mutiny, it was imperative that Kev found a new way of getting in and out of the show. Happily for me, he took to a three-hander of my invention called The Thickies about a gaggle of harmless misfits with balaclavas on their heads and nothing much between their ears. They weren't based on anyone in particular (so the members of Pan's People could sleep easy), just the kind of folk you overhear in cafes and at bus stops, having conversations like:-

LEN: Is it cold in here or is it me?

DAVID: No, it's not just you. We're here and all.

TRACEY: If you're cold, why don't you put something on?

LEN: All right, I'll put the fire on.

DAVID: I've only just put it off.

TRACEY: How do you put a fire off?

LEN: You say, sorry fire, I can't go out with you tonight, I've got to wash my hair.

TRACEY: How can you wash your hair with that balaclava on?

DAVID: No, he's pretending.

LEN: I'm not pretending. I really have got a balaclava on.

Forget calling them The Thickies, they should have been dubbed The Ramblers' Association. I was thrilled that these pieces of surreal verbage were seen by a decent amount of people at 8pm on a Saturday. Before *3OAK* was invented, that slot was the almost exclusive preserve of *The Two Ronnies*, always a mums-and-dads sort of show that the kids watched too but only because they didn't have hoodies to play with and x-boxes to wear.

Don't get me wrong: I was a big fan of the Ronnies in their first few seasons (and loved Barker's all-but-forgotten radio sketch show, *Lines From My Grandfather's Forehead)*. These days though, Barker and Corbett are either national treasures or sacred cows, I forget which. Anyway, a law has been passed which forbids any criticism of their interminable reign, conveniently overlooking the fact that by 1982, Ronnies B and C were starting to look like a pair of embarrassing granddads at a fancy dress do, impersonating Kid Creole and Boy George respectively, even though we could all see their crows' feet through the make-up.

Now, I'm not suggesting for one paragraph that many *3OAK* moments weren't every bit as ropey as the Ronnies at their worst, nor would I presume to say we gained a special place in the nation's hearts, lungs or even legs. My point is this: for the first time, a bunch of young things had produced a peak BBC1 Saturday night comedy show for another bunch of young things to watch - and we didn't care what their parents thought of it…which could be why it was axed after three series and a Christmas special.

Q: How many actors does it take to fuck up a punchline?

A: How many has Equity got?

5

NO ONE LEAVES THIS ROOM TILL THEY'VE THOUGHT OF SOMETHING FUNNY

" It's funnay…but it's not me."

Actually, that wasn't why. We'd all had enough. The cast were ready to pursue solo projects (well, two of them were) and Kev had plans for the rest of us. A new, late-night, live topical series was in the works, fronted by a star whose identity was a closely guarded secret. All we knew was that he was used to doing live TV and had some kind of connection with the music business. We began to think Billy Cotton might be making a comeback…or maybe it was Billy Connolly who started his career on the folk-club circuit, then in a band called The Humblebums alongside Gerry Rafferty.

Eventually, after the ink on the contract had been duly smudged, we were allowed to know that our new playmate was a man named Bob Davis who called himself Jasper Carrott. His first words to me were...

JASPER: My name's Bob too.

ME: Is it really, Bob?

JASPER: Call me Jasper.

Having excelled in the live idiom on LWT where he famously brought a telly on stage, changed channels and spontaneously took the piss out of what was on the other side, Bob...sorry, Jasper...was determined to prove that he could cut it on the senior network with scripts of a 'sardonic' nature (his word).

Seizing on the fact that we could be bang up-to-date, Kev decided to recruit a couple of crusading journalists renowned for their ability to break controversial stories before the regular press got hold of them. These they could feed directly to the writers, which had the added advantage of saving us from having to read crap newspapers. When I say 'us', I mean me, Rob Grant and Doug Naylor, Kim Fuller and hair-twiddling Tony Sarchet. And when I say 'a couple of crusading journalists', I mean Duncan Campbell and Ian Hislop. One of these was highly diligent in his efforts on our behalf while the other preferred to channel his energies into becoming a magazine editor.

Initially, Ben Elton was going to be with us and he attended our preliminary meeting where he spoke at length about what a fantastic opportunity and privilege it would be to be working on this programme with such a wonderful team. He then went off to write *The Young Ones* and we never saw him again.

The approach to scripting *Carrott's Lib* as it was entitled, differed radically from *Three of a Kind* in, at the most, one respect. We were compelled to sit together in a windowless BBC conference room and not leave till we'd thought of something funny.

YOU: But that was your job!

...you cry, not without some degree of

accuracy. But to me, writing's a bit like wanking: you don't want to be seen doing it in front of your colleagues. And you certainly don't want to see them at it in front of you.

I know: the Americans do it this way all the time. Writing, that is, not wanking (although…) but damn it all, we were British with a centuries-old tradition of repression and embarrassment to our credit. I don't think any of us <u>really</u> liked working this way but while the others bore it with fortitude, I flicking hated it and couldn't wait to skulk away into a quiet corner and scribble out something on my own, only sharing it when I was convinced of its readiness.

YOU: What was your problem, Bob?

Glad you asked me. It was this: team shows are, by their nature, competitive and no one's going to laugh at your stuff if they think it might then get in the script and replace something of theirs. Also, Mr. Carrott was a five-star bugger to write for. It wasn't his fault, but just about everything we came up with in those early days was greeted with the same response :-

JASPER: It's funnay…but it's not me.

He was a Brummie, you know.

And he was right. Nobody could do Carrott lines quite like Carrott and he'd had enough years of proving it on stage, in clubs and on ITV. Even Barry Cryer, who swelled the numbers on a subsequent series, *Carrott Confidential*, told me he struggled to crack Jasper's style - and Barry had written successfully for such awkward sods…I mean, such idiosyncratic characters as Frankie Howerd and Tommy Cooper (among about a thousand others).

Aware of this greatly discouraging factor in my heart of hearts, I resolved to make myself useful - and justify the portion of the licence-fee being spent on me - by knocking out a few sketches for the supporting cast.

This led me to lampoon the SDP (Social Democrat Party) 'roadshow', a hilarious event where the razzmatazz of American-style politics provided a wholly incongruous framework for the less-than-glitzy figures of Shirley Williams and Roy Jenkins. These were the days when honourable members started crossing the line into showbiz with mixed results: a mix of tragedy and disaster. A David Steele speech was sampled on a dance track and Neil Kinnock guested on a Tracey Ullman pop video before trying his hand at stand-up (with my help, God help me) but I can't talk of that in a book that's meant to be about comedy. I believe someone provided a similar gag-writing service for Tony Blair in the '90s (with equally ghastly results, no doubt, the man being seemingly…incapable of de-livering…a sentence without…pausing after every…three words) and of course, in the 21st century, just about every failed MP gets to present a show on train journeys or become a human floor-mop on *Strictly Come Dancing*. Then there are the authors: our pals at Westminster have produced many works of great fiction (better known as their expenses) but at the time of *Carrott's Lib*, sketches like 'The SDP Middle-of-the-Road Show' did have some novelty value. Still, I didn't exactly strike gold there.

The only time I felt I struck as much as bronze was when I gave them a thing called 'The Facts of Work', set in a secondary school classroom. Unemployment was around three million then and I hoped this piece might go down well enough to prevent it becoming three million and one.

TEACHER: Now class, we've all reached a responsible age where I think we can talk sensibly about…work.

CLASS: [SNIGGERING]

TEACHER: That's enough! There is nothing dirty or smutty about work. Now can anyone tell me where jobs come from?

KID 1: Sir, from under a gooseberry bush.

KID 2: No sir, the stork brings 'em.

KID 3: No sir, you get 'em from the Job Centre.

TEACHER [APPALLED]: That's kids' stuff! You don't still believe that, do you? No, for a job to happen, a worker and an employer have to, well, sort of…get together and…well, if you turn to page 43 of your text books, you'll see diagrams of some of the basic positions for getting work.

[KIDS LOOK AT 'THE JOY OF WORK']

KID 4: Look, this one's on his knees!

TEACHER: Yes, that one's known as the 'Submissionary Position' with the employer on top. But they can change places.

Steve Frost was tremendous as the teacher and the others made entertaining if slightly over-age kids.

Throughout the run, Steve and his double-act partner Mark Arden provided a youthful and surreal counterpoint to Carrott's observational monologues. As The Oblivion Boys, they were much respected and enjoyed on London's then fledgling comedy club circuit and deserved to do easily as well as Ade & Rik but it didn't quite happen for them. Instead, they became best known for their creative and splendidly silly Carling Black Label ads, especially the *Dam Busters* piss-take.

In fact, Rik Mayall did perform (rather than appear) in the first Carrott series in a serial he wrote with his partner, Lise Mayer. 'Dave The Cardboard Box' was every bit as thrilling as its name suggests. For three endless minutes each week, the unseen Rik described the 'action' as we were treated to the sight of a cardboard box that, understandably, did nothing. And that was the joke, such as it was. The rest of us tried to persuade Kev that the emperor had never had a finer set of new clothes but he was in awe of Rik and kept faith with the item. He probably thought our grapes had gone sour but no, we wanted 'Dave' pulped for one reason alone: it was crap. What Mr. Carrott himself thought of it I can't recall but it was still early days for him. He felt he had something to prove and perhaps he didn't want to rock the BBC boat (plenty of time for that later).

Both press and public reaction to the programme were good - an unusual pairing in my experience. Even Margaret Forwood in *The Sun* liked us, despite Mr. Carrott's determination to make *Sun* reader jokes replace Irish ones in the nation's psyche. He had a personal gripe with the paper over some old article where they'd rubbished him and we were only too happy to jump on the anti-*Sun* band wagon, hating its Thatcherite politics as we all did. This was just after the Falklands war when they'd used the headline…

SUN: GOTCHA!

…after the *SS Belgrano* sank. Suddenly,

newspapers were editorialising when they should have been reporting and Screaming Blue Murdoch's sheet (not the word but it's close) was by far the worst offender.

Jasper's take on politics was officially neutral. By nature he was a conservative with a small c. The tone of the show, though, was politically correct with a large PC, mainly due to overly-developed ideological consciences in certain corners of the writers' room. I remember (with no fondness at all) one seemingly endless group discussion over a joke involving Smarties. Somewhere in the script was a mention of brown ones and, unbelievably, we all sat there pondering whether this could be misinterpreted as a reference to black people. You might think a bunch of adults could have used their time more productively but we are talking about media folk here.

To an extent, the show's script editor, Script Ed, was the voice of reason on series one. He was our daddy figure, having worked on *TW3* and *The Frost Report* among many, so he was really the only one who knew what he was doing. All that was to change come series two when Ed had just quit smoking and taken up being arsey. He clung to the view that everything had to be explained very obviously to the BBC1 audience, that we needed to…

ED: …lead them by the hand.

(a euphemism for 'treat them like spit-dribbling cretins') and as far as Ed was concerned, you either agreed with him or you were wrong. Us young 'uns resented this - but quietly, in case he heard. Only Doug Naylor had the balls to challenge him at one point with the simple remark…

DOUG: I don't agree with you.

Ed was struck dumb by this - almost - but managed to come back with…

ED: But you <u>can't</u> not agree with me!

Still, sometimes the committee structure of our working lives yielded fruit of pure gold (you can see why I never became a novelist). On the 1983 election special, the entire writing team (minus one) sat down in Carrott's Brighton hotel suite - he was gigging in the town that night - and bashed out one of the best monologues I've ever seen him do. The theme was 'virgin voters', people who were 'doing it' for the first time and included classics like...

JASPER: It's not the size of your cross that matters, it's where you put it.

The pay-off had a touch of genius: by this stage, the virgin voter is worried that, by not taking precautions, he might have got the country into trouble. The parallel of an unwanted progeny culminated in the line...

JASPER: One thing's certain: it'll be an ungrateful bastard.

That year, Margaret Thatcher was re-elected with a landslide. 'Nuff said.

The reason I'm able to lavish such praise on the voter monologue without boasting is that I didn't write any of it. I was that 'minus one', working on another sketch up at the TV Centre concrete doughnut, thereby missing the monologue writing session altogether.

It wasn't the only masterpiece on view that night. Emma Thompson made her one appearance on the show as a sort of Lady Olga Maitland figure. Historians will recall that the anti-nuclear Greenham Common women were then a small but surprisingly sharp thorn in the government's side and Lady O, the honourable member for Sutton and Cheam (though I doubt if Tony Hancock would have voted for her) struck back with her Women For Defence collective, earning herself the soubriquet of the Duchess of Nuke Street. In James Hendrie's brilliantly satirical rallying speech, Emma's cut-glass campaigner proudly declared…

EMMA: There are over two thousand names on our petition…or four thousand if you ignore the hyphens.

The TV Theatre audience erupted…

and I like to think people at home might have done a bit of surreptitious erupting in the privacy of their own front rooms. Not everyone voted Tory that day; it just seemed like it.

Mention of the TV Theatre reminds me that we were lucky enough to have escaped the concrete doughnut's unatmospheric bog-standard studios. Instead, the BBC had installed us in a proper entertainment venue with a strong pedigree. Previously, it had been the Shepherd's Bush Empire, a title it reclaimed some time in the 1990s. Sadly for our audiences, most of the shows went out in the depths of winter and the uniformed jobsworths forced them to freeze their bits off while queuing in the not-so-great outdoors. Still, at least a sideshow of sorts was provided by an actor who'd enjoyed small-screen success in an ITV detective series. Although he was dating one of our cast, it seems the jobsworths wouldn't let him in either, so he habitually paraded up and down in front of the punters, trying desperately to get recognised. Poor chap, most of them probably took him for a ticket tout.

His girlfriend didn't make it to series two and neither did Kev who'd scored such a winner with *The Young Ones* that he'd been poached by LWT. Over there, the pay was so good that one ex-BBC producer who joined them looked at his starting salary and thought it was the date.

Taking over at the Carrott helm was Geoff Posner who'd done such a terrific job directing series one. He had an immense flair for making stuff leap off the screen at you: literally, a man of vision. In his new capacity as producer, Geoff was determined to keep the original writing team together. He didn't mind a few welcome additions (including Andrea Solomons) but he balked at the thought of subtractions. This was bad news for me as I really didn't think I could face another seven weeks of debating the ideological soundness of brown Smarties. Besides, I was getting no nearer to cracking Jasper's syntax and felt strongly that I wouldn't be missed. Geoff was having none of it and called an emergency writers' meeting to persuade me to stay. All very flattering but the last thing I wanted. Being a man of steely resolve, I caved in and spent the autumn wishing I hadn't.

The first edition of the second series had as its guests The Animals, recently reformed after over a decade of acrimonious separation. It was good to know that time hadn't healed a thing as the vitriolic exchanges between Eric Burdon and Alan Price carried from their dressing-room all the way down the corridor and straight into our ears. There's nothing quite like the sound of two rock legends swearing at each other in fluent Geordie…and at least it took our minds off the latest variation on the brown Smarties debate.

And, for that matter, the behaviour of our star. With Kev gone, there was no one senior enough to keep him in order and he fell into the habit of wanting to be right about everything. Don't ask me why a multi-millionaire celebrity felt the need to assert himself over a bunch of unknown ex-students with two-finger typing skills but perhaps he was suffering from what we doctors call PS syndrome. PS was a short impressionist with a matching TV career who filled the prime Saturday slot for half an hour on half a dozen occasions. At one point in rehearsal, he brought proceedings to a standstill by yelling...

PS: Am I the only one working on this show who hasn't got a fucking degree?!

The answer to that was almost certainly...

DEGREE HOLDERS: Yes.

...but on a comedy show, what does that matter?

It could be that Mr. Carrott was turning a bit chippy towards us for the same reason but whatever was causing it, he just had to prove his point. One day, his point was that show 7 was going to be a flop. As we were only preparing for show 3 at this stage and every week we began with a clean slate, we were somewhat non-plussed at the idea that anyone other than Madame Petulengro could predict the failure of show 7. But no, Bob Davis was insistent.

```
JASPER: Show 3 will be fine.
Shows 4 and 5, they'll be
okay, not worried about them,
not worried about show 6.
It's show 7, that's the one
we've got to watch out for.
Definitely the danger zone.
```

Well, that was the gist anyway.

Something else happened early in that series which inadvertently set a pattern. What with one sketch and another, we hadn't got round to cobbling Jasper's mid-show monologue together until Friday night; not good when there was a mere day to go before transmission. At times though, the adrenalin (or maybe just the fear) carries you through and this one turned out to be as well-received as the virgin voter routine. Shame, really. If it hadn't been, we'd have got our Friday nights back - but now Jasper was convinced that because it worked this way once, it'd necessarily work the same way every week. Despite this theory being disproved on several subsequent Fridays, he still wouldn't budge and we ended up burning our comedy candles at both ends as well as in the middle.

Mind you, the general trend of the series was upward. The press were still with us: the *Express* even quoted a line I'd given to Nick Maloney who was playing the FBI's top man, J. Edgar in a JFK anniversary sketch. His opening sally was…

NICK: I'm Hoover. I beat as I sweep as I clean.

In fact, *Carrott's Lib* was such a success that Geoff picked up a BAFTA for it before the end of the second run.

But then came show 7. Looking at a fading video of the episode nearly three decades on, I can't see any immediate disaster signals. He was delivering the monologues more or less flawlessly, using his admirable ability to read an autocue without appearing to do so. He was so good at this that we tended to forget there was a script at all. At one point, there's a totally excusable stumble over the word 'aniseed'; no other hiccups, though. Then we reach the final sketch, a faux sitcom featuring the rest of the cast as the archetypal nuclear family awaiting the government all-clear on contamination at Windscale. Government official (Jasper) duly arrives, has one line, containing not just the punch-line to the sketch but also the last laugh of the programme…and he buggers it up. Cue end credits and playout music - and a somewhat bemused audience.

JASPER: Well, I told you it would happen.

…was the best he could manage at the after-show curry. As apologies go, it didn't even come. It seems so absurd to be angry over something so trivial, but we were - and it's downright preposterous that so gifted and normally professional a comic should have allowed himself to go down with such a virulent bout of hubris in front of millions But that assumes he blew the gag on purpose - and nobody's that insecure…are they?

Thank God (or BBC1's Programme Controller), there was still a Christmas special to go. With any luck, *Carrott's Lib* might redeem itself.

If memory serves, it did…and blow me down a lamp-post at the corner of the street, I even managed to get a couple of lines into his monologues: one about people, on the eve of 1984, thinking Orwell was Keith Harris's duck and another describing a one-to-one relationship as something you have at 12:59. Maybe I'd finally cracked that Carrott style, but probably not. In any case, it was a bit late for that: the series ended, our ways parted and he came back a year later with a different set of writers on a show called *Carrott Confidential*. Actually, it was the same bottle with a new label but its star no longer had anything to prove. He'd shown the nation - and himself - that he could do live 'sardonic' humour on the BBC.

I learned a lot doing *Carrott's Lib*. Despite the grimitude of conference room weekdays and pointlessly late Friday sessions, I wouldn't have missed those Saturday nights at the TV Theatre. Even so, the actor in me knows that being in a live show is nowhere near as nerve-racking as watching from the wings. If you're 'on' when something goes wrong, there's a chance you might be able to rescue it…or, I suppose, make it worse. Anything's better than standing by helplessly as your sketch dies from lack of laughs or a buggered-up punch-line.

In recent years, Tina Fey's dazzlingly good *30 Rock* has reflected this genre with hilarious accuracy, her years on *Saturday Night Live* paying dividends. At the time of *Carrott's Lib*, a movie called *My Favourite Year* did the same, featuring a fictionalised version of Sid Caesar's *Show of Shows*, a TV series similar to ours in 1950s America. A bunch of us went to see it and were particularly struck by an early scene where, as the writers and star wrestle over the fate of the opening monologue, a floor assistant gives a running commentary to the director in the box, consisting of…

FLOOR ASSISTANT: Monologue's out.

…then, a few seconds later…

FLOOR ASSISTANT: Monologue's in.

…shortly followed by…

FLOOR ASSISTANT: Monologue's out again.

We all laughed. Uncomfortably.

Q: What's the sound of one hand clapping?

A: Monday night, first house, Glasgow Empire.

6

HENRY THE FIRST

"The best thing about writing Lenny Henry's show for Radio One was it meant we could take the piss out of...Radio One.".

Having quit the TV jungle for the relative safety of the radio woodland, I was glad to see everything had changed. The place no longer resembled some small corner of the '50s with stills of Peter Brough (literally, Archie Andrews's support act), Ted Ray and the Huggets festooning the functional corridors. Instead, it all smacked of the swinging era, the stills now representing Tony Blackburn, Ed 'Stewpot' Stewart and Dave Lee Travis Perkins. Really quite modern...for 1982.

There was a simple explanation: I was in another building, Light Ent having given way to Radio One as my means of crust-making. The happy, happy sound of the nation's favourite station had a new recruit in the towering form of Lenworth George Henry who, between series of *Three of a Kind*, had been given the chance to DJ on a show called *The Sunday Hoot*. I forget which day it was on.

Kim Fuller, Tony Sarchet and I were drafted in to help Lenny gag up the bits between the records (to use a technical term), much to the bemusement of the producer, fifty percent of whose name was Dave. A hardened warhorse of the *Radio One Roadshow* and Peter Powell's drive-time sequence, Dave saw no need for writers on the network, arguing that young Mr. Powell never used any. That much was clear just from listening to Peter's show, but we kept that observation to ourselves. Happily for us, Lenny was able to overrule his resident Rottie and the fun began, for us if not for Dave.

One of the best things about writing a show for Radio One was that it enabled us to take the piss out of…

Radio One. This would have been a largely redundant exercise on Radio Four whose listeners probably thought the pirate boats were still going, or on BBC1 whose viewers didn't know radio was still going. Lenny's skills as an impressionist led us to parody John Peel, Paul Gambaccini, Simon Bates (tougher to fake that sincerity than you might think), Andy Peebles, Tommy Vance and the marvellous if grumpy John Walters, a hard voice to capture without straying into Peel, probably due to the two Johns spending so much time together that they were practically joined at the beergut.

With surprisingly few exceptions, these verbal caricatures of Britain's best-loved DJs (and Andy Peebles) were taken in good part, though I do recall Annie Nightingale - then still only half of the station's female presenters - quaking lest she might be next (we spared her that) and Dave Lee Travis Perkins tersely enquiring:-

DLTP: Who's he ripping the piss out of this week?!

...but then he was, famously, similarly disgruntled nearly a decade later when Paul Whitehouse and Harry Enfield fed the entire jock world to the lions as, respectively, Smashie and Nicey.

When it came to Jimmy Savile, whose programme followed ours, it would have been too obvious for Lenny to do a straightforward impersonation, though he'd have been more than capable of it. Instead, on the suggestion of the brilliant James Hendrie, I got into the habit of pre-hearing the first few inches of Savile's tape ahead of transmission, copying down his opening remarks and handing them to Lenny who would end his show thus:-

```
LEN: And now here's Jimmy
Savile to say, 'Now then, now
then, how's about that then,
guys and gals, where were you
twenty years ago this week?'
```

...after which, the veteran broadcaster would obligingly repeat these words verbatim. What Lord Arthur's favourite son himself thought of this is not documented, but his producer left us in no doubt of his own disapproval by barking down the phone so loudly that he was still all too audible when the receiver was held at arm's length. His main objection seemed to be that we'd blown the gaff on Jimmy's prog being pre-recorded (as if anyone cared - it was an oldies show, after all).

As I said, though, this negativity was the minority view at Radio One where most of the presenters were supportive. Peely and Gambo (how did they think of those nicknames?) even went to the trouble of appearing in a couple of sketches themselves (and it probably was a trouble as I'm pretty sure they never got paid). Occasionally a DJ voice would prove too difficult, even for the dextrous Mr. H. Mike Read had the tones of a public schoolboy who'd knocked the corners off his consonants for the sake of rock cred but remained just a bit too bland to be replicated. A deft way round this was to feature clips of the real Read endlessly strumming his instrument on the breakfast show - as was his wont -

and present him as the subject of a mockumentary in the series *Guitar Greats*. This had the added advantage of giving Lenny the chance to 'do' Alexis Korner, host of the real *Guitar Greats* whose voice had about it an essence of baked sandpaper.

Luckily, the goodwill towards Lenny continued, but a black face in Broadcasting House was still a novelty then - outside of the canteen, of course - and this led to some toe-curling social gaffes.

In at number three, the production secretary who spent an inordinate interval gawping at Lenny. When he noticed this, she quickly covered herself with the words...

SEC: Er...just looking. Never seen one up close before.

Bubbling under at two, the technical operator (posh term for engineer) who asked Lenny if he wanted his coffee white or...and left it at that, unable to bring himself to say 'black'.

And riding high in that all-important number one spot, the Radio One executive who invited Lenny to dinner and...well, it went like this:-

EXEC: Shall we put a date in the book?

LEN: I need to check my diary. I'm so busy right now, I barely have time for a bath.

EXEC: You'll never get white that way.

The gentleman concerned went on to be a network controller. Serves him right.

The Sunday Hoot lived up to its title far better in series two (summer 1983). For a start, it really did take place on a Sunday as Lenny was let loose live and self-op (playing the uncompact discs himself) in contrast to the earlier safety of weekday pre-recordings. Secondly, it came a lot closer to being a hoot when Dave left us to spend more time with Peter Powell. He was replaced by a mild-mannered young Beatles fan called

Kevin Howlett who clearly had a different approach to the comedy 'creatives'. He actually seemed pleased to see us. As a result, Tony, Kim and I were happier and produced far better material than before. We began to feel more at home, less like audio vagrants (there was probably a band of that name on the Peel show).

Liveness - one of the best things about being live is that stuff goes wrong. After a successful opening half-hour in which Lenny, self-op for the first time, without the aid of dual controls, didn't misflick a single switch, news time arrived in its own inevitable way and a headline-hungry nation heard Mr. Henry introduce that day's bulletin boy as Batthew Mannister. Unlike the resultantly corpsing Lenworth, Batthew Mannister didn't bat a lid, but clearly stored the incident in his mental dossier, for ten years later he wrought a fearful vengeance on Radio One by becoming its controller, sacking all the jocks and providing an audience of listening millions...for Radio Two.

Of the script team, I was the one most fired up by the show's live element. I loved coming into BH every Sunday, breakfasting with Lenny and Kevin on the eighth floor (because that's where the food was) and hobnobbing with wireless legend David Jacobs as he polished his vowels in readiness for a *Melodies for You* transmission on Radio Two. Most hacks don't get out of bed before noon (the show's finishing time) but my presence was required to feed 'Trevor MacDoughnut' (do you see what he did there?) with a string of news item gags culled from the Sunday red-tops. Not much time to think, then: just how I like it. I never was one for thinking. Lenny had perfected his version of the UK's best-known newscaster during the *Tiswas* era (a frantic Saturday morning kids' telly show that exuded fun in a way its BBC rivals never managed) but he was just as keen on developing new characters from his own imagination. Foremost among these was Delbert Wilkins - the Brixton wide-boy soon to become a TV fixture - and a supercool record producer given to 'Valley speak' whom I christened Con Dominium.

The language of the San Fernando valley was first exploited for comic purposes by Moon Unit Zappa, the imaginatively-named daughter of Frank, on her single *Valley Girl*, a Lenny favourite and worth a Google today (other search engines are available). The song included such expressions as 'bitchen' (good), 'grody' (bad), 'grody to the max' (really quite revolting) and 'toadally' (totally).

Although frequently 'dragged up' most effectively on TV, Lenny was happier cross-dressing on radio, saving himself hours of make-up, wardrobe prep and the need to wear tights. It was still (just about) the era of BBC tea-ladies pushing their trolleys round the corridors and engaging celebs and filing clerks alike in flirty banter. They've all gone now, of course, replaced by vending machines from the exotic climes of an industrial estate in

Kidderminster. Lenny's creation was the bombastic Elfrieda who would interrupt whatever was being transmitted at 10.15, be it a Henry quip or an Elvis Costello album track.

A less frequent but equally female visitor rejoiced in the name of Babbalonia Johnson, ostensibly a *National Enquirer* gossip hack who came up with titbits like:-

```
BABBALONIA: Good news for
those who can lip-read: Mick
Jagger's just had War & Peace
printed on his.
```

For her voice, Lenny pulled off the clever trick of keeping it low and husky while never descending into the masculine range: a tough call for a bloke who's 6 foot 4.

Later, when required to dress as Babbalonia for TV, he'd get in touch with his masculine side between takes by hitching up his frock and declaring:-

```
LEN [BROAD YORKS]: I'm a man,
I drink 15 pints a night and I
```

After the excitement of live Sunday morning shows, fun-loving Radio One decided less was more...so they paid us less and saved more. The result was a switch to Saturday lunchtimes, a shorter show and a midweek pre-record. Though Lenny didn't seem perturbed by this, the *Hoot* inevitably lost its edge; knowing you can go back and erase any blunders has an enervating effect on your performance, as any relationship counsellor will tell you.

From my point of view, it meant no more topical jokes from that day's scandal sheets. If only Fleet Street could have brought out their Saturday papers three days early.

Eventually, Lenny and Radio One embarked on a trial separation that's continued ever since. He told me they hadn't quite appreciated what kind of presenter he'd be. They thought they were getting another Afternoon

Boy. This was a reference to one of the weekday line-up who had accosted Lenny and me outside the production office one day, oozing praise for *Three of a Kind* before accusing us of basing one of our characters on a routine from his show! I assured him this was impossible...as none of us had ever heard his show.

I thought I'd finished with Radio One but it hadn't finished with me. Later in the decade, I popped up for a while on Janice Long's mid-evening programme, spouting topical one-liners in between records by The Disease and The Cure (for some reason), then became a contributor to Adrian Juste's long-running Saturday spree. This was unlike anything else on the network but it did remind me of Jack Jackson's long-gone *Record Roundabout* where the former bandleader would intersperse clips from *Steptoe and Son*, *The Frost Report* and *Till Death Us Do Part* to create sketches in which the characters from these seemed to be talking to each other and to him.

Adrian's show took it a stage further and introduced hitherto unheard comics like the American surrealists Steven Wright and Emo Phillips (to the delight of the new British breed such as Dominic Holland) as well as custom-made topical sketches, which is where I and the other writers (including Eric Merriman and Stuart Silver) came in.

Mr. Juste's fame at Radio One made him a hot property for the British Forces Network whose output could be heard more or less worldwide (a big deal before the days of the internet) and we collaborated on a number of Bank Holiday specials for them, along with gifted actresses like Kate Smart, Lorraine Murrin and Rebecca Front. Rebecca's subsequent TV fame on *The Day Today*, *Lewis* and *The Thick Of It* is well-deserved and we could tell how good she was from the start. In a 60-second version of *Sunset Boulevard* (complete with chillingly apt incidental music provided by Adrian), I was William Holden to Rebecca's Gloria Swanson while Adrian appeared as

Erich Von Stroheim.

SWANSON: Young man, write me the greatest script of my career and I'll give you my body.

HOLDEN: No deal.

SWANSON: Ok, write me the greatest script of my career <u>or</u> I'll give you my body.

HOLDEN: I'll do it, I'll do it!

SWANSON: Max, show him to my room.

STROHEIM: Yes, madam.

<u>F/X: SQUEAKY DOOR</u>

SWANSON: And stop making that noise! He needs oiling, you know.

HOLDEN: The butler?

SWANSON: Yes. He used to be my husband.

HOLDEN: Good career move.

PRODUCER: I think I know what your script needs.

WRITER: What's that?

PRODUCER: Something to make it funny.

7

HENRY THE SECOND

"I had yet to learn that the two most important words when addressing a star were 'wonderful' and 'darling' in that order."

It was time for Lenny to go back to TV where his own series awaited. But what to call it? One Of A Kind? Henry The First? No (thank God) but the working title of 'The Lenny Henry Comedy Selection' didn't exactly transport me and I said so, going so far as to opine that it sounded like a slightly dodgy con-fectionery assortment. Bold in those days, I had yet to learn that the two most important words when addressing a star were 'wonderful' and 'darling' in that order.

Less than delighted at this challenge to his authority, our leader spat back,

LEN: Can you think of anything better?

Happily, I could and replied,

ME: How about The Lenny Henry
Show?

It was a moment of genius.
How did I come up with it? Naturally,
it was adopted instantly and won me a
Bafta Gold in the Best Title For A
Light Entertainment Show With Lenny
Henry In It category. Mind you, I'd be
tempted to say it compares
unfavourably with the more recent
Lenny Henry in Pieces if it weren't for the
fact that I didn't think of that one.
Aside from this masterstroke of title
conceit, I don't recall a great deal about
the series. This probably means I didn't
contribute much to it, despite accepting
a nice wedge of licence-payers' money
to have my name on the credits.
I do remember being stuck in the same
conference room where many jokes
were born and even more died in the
name of *Carrott's Lib*, surrounded by

most of the same faces; only those of Grant and Naylor were missing. According to the history books, French & Saunders and that other fine double-act, Jimmy Nail and Nicholas Lyndhurst were among the guests, along with that redoubtable star of stage musicals, Bertice Redding. I'd last encountered her on roller skates (her, not me) singing *You've Got The Right Key But The Wrong Keyhole* on the same edition of the Russell Harty show that featured Maureen Lipman's Thatcher monologue and David Steele, the disgruntled chorister.

This time, Bernice, in more health-and-safety-friendly footwear, played Lenny's mum in a spectacularly accurate (and really quite funny) pastiche of the famous Michael Jackson *Thriller* video, entitled 'Thinner'. Kim Fuller wrote the main lyric in which an anorexic Michael was getting 'thinner' because he wouldn't eat his 'dinner'. That rhyming dictionary in the corner of the office was starting to pay for itself. I added the middle section, spoken by Lenny in his best Vincent Price:-

LEN: Young Michael is his mother's pride

But he also has a darker side.
By day, he glows with health and fitness;

At night, he's a Jehovah's Witness.

The only other sketch that leaps to mind involved a reunion with Radio One's Paul Gambaccini, a man more prepared to send himself up than his earnest on-air persona would have you believe. Kim and I co-wrote 'The History of Rock' wherein Gambo spoke reverentially of The Mersey Sound which, in 1961, was the hooter on the Birkenhead ferry. As you might suppose, Lenny was in it too, portraying a range of pop icons including both Jimi Hendrix and his manager Chas Chandler who claimed to be so close to the star that…

LEN (AS CHAS): When he played the guitar with those teeth, well, they were MY teeth!

The reason this looked so good was because the director (Geoff Posner again - was he the only one they had?) brought his *Top of the Pops* grounding to the table. Previously, it had stood him in good stead on *Not The Nine* when shooting 'Nice Video, Shame About The Song'. If a pop piss-take's going to work, it has to look right. There's nothing less hip than a bunch of comics trying to ape a medium they don't understand. It's just not with it, daddyo.

After series one of the superbly-titled *Lenny Henry Show*, I was all sketched out. Having written for so many revue series from '79 to '85, I felt they'd all begun to merge into one. Maybe they were all one, a humungous sketch conglomerate called 'Not Alas Three Of A Kick Up The Carrott's Comedy Selection'. For my next project, I decided to take the list of ninety-three writers and reduce it by ninety-two.

ACTOR: Is there a doctor in the house?

DOCTOR: Yes. Why?

ACTOR: Can you make this script better?

8

I SPY WITH MY LITTLE GUY

"Writing the lyrics was one thing, but I was ill-equipped to compose the music, being both tone-deaf and tune-dumb."

The best way to do this was to give up earning a living and go into the theatre. Thanks to the good offices of a writer-performer called Stewart Permutt, I was able to get my foot in the woodworm-infested door of London's most prestigious (and most delapidated) fringe venue, The King's Head, Islington.

It sounds like a pub...because it is one. But beyond the well-preserved Victorian bar complete with matching 'old money' - the staff quaintly ask for your cash in pounds, shillings and pence yet still expect the decimal equivalent - lies what used to be known as a function room. This unprepossessing space, where half the seating is at right-angles to the stage ensuring an outbreak of tennis-watcher's neck among the punters, has played host to some spectacular theatrical triumphs - and mine.

The Iron Curtain Call was somewhere between a play and a musical, betraying my roots in what used to be called 'revue' and what was just as often misspelt as 'review'. If ever a 'theatrical review' was advertised, I'd avoid it in case they'd got it right and it involved a bunch of critics on stage.

No, this was a revue based on the format popularized by the Cambridge University Footlights Club and featuring three characters who, while never having performed for the Footlights Club, did attend Cambridge University en route to their final destination of Moscow.

```
[THREE URBANE YOUNG MEN IN
'30s DINNER SUITS ENTER AND
SING:-]
```

```
ALL:      We're perfect English
                     gentlemen,

          A cut above the rest,

PHILBY: But we're shortly going
                East    which    means
        This country will go West.

MacLEAN:    Still, our flawless
                         etiquette

          Has never failed us yet.
BURGESS: We always cock our
                     little finger

          When we tell a lie.

ALL:      Cambridge has societies

          In which we are intruders.

BURGESS: I got in the Apostles
                              Club

          Because I'm so like Judas.

PHILBY:      But although we're
                     total frauds,

          We still watch the Test at
                              Lords

MacLEAN:And we're awf'lly good
                         at games

             Like  'I  spy  with  my
                     little Guy'.
```

Writing the lyrics was one thing, but I was ill-equipped to compose the music, being both tone-deaf and tune-dumb. I approached Peter Brewis with whom I'd concocted a few topical numbers for *Carrott's Lib*, but he'd served his time in fringe theatre and didn't see returning to poverty as a smart career move. In fact, Peter was only too happy to step down and make way for an older man.

At 75, Geoffrey Wright was certainly that. My first sighting of him on Stowmarket railway station put me in mind of William Mervyn in his 'kindly old gentleman' role from Lionel Jeffries's movie of *The Railway Children*. Geoffrey was rather less of a portly old gentleman than the actor but was instantly recognisable as a benign force. He managed to pass on his considerable experience and wisdom without any of that when-you've-been-in-this-business-as-long-as-I-have kind of tosh you get from some older hands.

And what experience! This man

had actually written many of the melodies for the original 1930s Footlights revues, rubbing shoulders with a fellow undergraduate named Nigel Burgess (author, ironically, of the number *He's Nice, He's Clean, He's British*). The reason this is ironic won't be lost on you if I say Nigel's older brother was called Guy. According to Geoffrey, although Burgess major wasn't involved in Footlights shows himself, he would occasionally swan in with an imperious air and cast a watchful eye over the talent (all of it male).

During his student days, Geoffrey also met the fourth man, Anthony Blunt but never had the remotest clue as to what he, Burgess and the second and third men were up to. Ten years later, in wartime, Blunt introduced him to the third man, Kim Philby (so beautifully played in the movie by Orson Welles). With hindsight, Geoffrey concluded that the pair had been sounding him out with a view to possible Soviet recruitment. The fact that this only dawned on him after Blunt was exposed in 1979 suggests that, unlike his near-namesake Peter, this Mr. Wright wasn't cut out to be a spycatcher.

In the post-war years, Geoffrey studied composition under Alan Rawsthorne (there's a gag there but it's too cheap even for me) and had his only symphony performed on the Third Programme, or Radio Three as it's unknown today. But the piece of his that kept those PRS cheques rolling in down the decades was *Transatlantic Lullaby*. It still gets the odd airing on Radio Two, though probably not sandwiched between Spruce Bringsteen and Coldplate on the Herbert O'Dreary show.

It might be hard to imagine such an old-school gent in the forefront of the brave new Royal Court Theatre movement of the mid-to-late '50s but there Geoffrey stood in the pit, conducting the band for the British premiere of *The Threepenny Opera* (starring Bill Owen and Warren Mitchell) as well as angry young John

Osborne's *The Entertainer*, a vehicle (that word again) for Laurence Olivier.

It's worth taking a moment to study Olivier's theatrical methods. I was told by a stage manager who'd worked with Larry on *A Long Day's Journey into Night* that each evening before curtain-up, Olivier would patrol the stage to re-orientate himself. One night, he returned to the wings and informed Phil that...

LARRY: The table has been set incorrectly.

PHIL [GLANCING AT TABLE]: I don't think it has.

LARRY: Oh yes. It's a good sixteenth-of-an-inch off its mark.

Phil duly checked the instructions on his groundplan, examined the table again and sure enough, it was indeed one sixteenth-of-an-inch off its mark. How in the name of Sir Herbert Beerbohm Tree did Larry know that?!

Meantime, back at *The Entertainer*, to aid his characterisation of fifth-rate turn

Archie Rice, Olivier had decided to insult the orchestra with personal remarks about their collective lack of hair. He was good enough to give Geoffrey Wright advance warning of this before strolling out at the preview and declaring...

LARRY [AS ARCHIE]: Cor blimey, look at them all down there. It's like playing to a box of bleedin' eggs!

Surprisingly, given that luvvies tend to close ranks against the outside world (musicians included), the supporting thesps felt the boys in the band were being unfairly pilloried and colluded with Geoffrey to serve Larry with a piping hot dish of oeuf sur le visage. Striding onto the boards come the press night, the great man of the theatre was a little non-plussed when his box-of-eggs quip went for nothing (gagspeak for 'didn't get a laugh'). Looking down, the reason became clear as he spotted one and all bedecked in bright ginger wigs. From the orchestral vantage point, it was possible to see the rest of the cast (Joan Plowright among them, according to Geoffrey) helpless with mirth at the momentary downfall of their leading player. Geoffrey felt obliged to apologise backstage but the star insisted it was...

LARRY: Perfectly all right, dear boy.

...in a clipped, brittle voice clearly indicating it was anything but.

So these were just some of the adventures that had befallen my new-found mentor. Initially, I'd only arranged to meet Geoffrey in a bid to learn more about the atmosphere in early 30s Cambridge and get a flavour of the kind of music in the shows. I certainly didn't think a man in his mid-70s with such a fine pedigree would be keen to start penning tunes for some tatty little fringe production where the term 'profit share' existed largely out of misplaced optimism. But when a trawl of all the Peter Brewises I knew resulted in a string of refusals, I felt I had nothing to lose by asking...

ME: Um, Geoffrey, I don't suppose for one minute you'd be interested but I'm looking for someone to write the music and...

GEOFFREY: Well, I was rather hoping you might say that, dear boy, because I've been working on one or two tunes...

[PRODUCES GROANING WEIGHT OF MANUSCRIPT SHEETS COVERED IN RECENTLY-ETCHED MINIMS AND QUAVERS.]

...and suddenly, I had a composer. Not just that but a composer able and willing to pastiche his own material. Who better to recreate the sound of an era than a man who'd helped create it in the first place?

I took it as an enormous compliment that he thought the project was good enough to be worth getting involved with. When interviewed by Capital Radio's Debbie Wolfe (daughter of Ronnie Wolfe, co-writer of *The Rag Trade*), Geoffrey generously said that had Guy Burgess been alive enough to drag himself over from Moscow and watch the show, it would probably have appealed to his sense of mischief. When the play was produced though, the sole survivor of the spy trio was Kim Philby…who <u>didn't</u> make it over from Moscow…for some reason.

As lunchtime productions go, I'd say we got a result. At least we made enough to buy lunch. Our all-singing, sometimes dancing company of three (all Richards: Denning, Frost and Cubison) were well-chosen and sympathetically directed by Kim Grant who had made me feel very important by including me in the casting process. This was the first time I'd ever been on the 'power' side of an audtion and I was intrigued to discover that you can pretty much tell whether an actor's right for the part the moment they step through the door. I've tried to remember this in subsequent years and always make a point of stepping through the door quite brilliantly.

Happily, the players, the director, our pianist Jonathan Gee and I all got on well and had some good-natured fun at the expense (literally) of our 'producer', a blubbery old gangland villain with much hair and few teeth who, about fifteen years later, ended his days with a bit part of the 'no acting required' kind in the movie *Lock, Stock And Two Smoking Barrels*. I was quite happy to sit the production out as far as performing went (two left feet and three right ones, you know) but I did join the troupe for a one-act companion piece when we transferred to the Offstage Downstairs in Chalk Farm, a small but swish theatre in the basement of a bookshop. By then, the part of Donald MacLean had been taken over by that marvellous and highly underrated character actor David Gooderson, best known as the pathologist in *A Touch Of Frost* (ah, the Jason connection again).

Our double-bill at the Offstage, known as *The Dirty Thirties*, paired *The Iron Curtain Call* with a solo piece about

Oswald Mosley in which I managed to look terrifyingly like the man (well, it certainly scared me) and even attempted to sing a spoof British Union of Fascists anthem with lyrics by me and music by Geoffrey. Okay, I sang it pretty badly, but I'm sure Mosley would have done the same, so let's call it excellent characterisation.

One source of great relief was that, as far as I know, no one who came to see me as Mosley got the wrong idea. The danger with presenting monsters of the far right in a satirical context is that thick people take it at face value. This happened frequently throughout the Alf Garnett years. When I met Garnett's creator, Johnny Speight, he told me Warren Mitchell was often hailed as a hero by racist thugs who thought he <u>was</u> Alf. This kind of response was also chillingly in evidence when Harry Enfield played the loathsome Loadsamoney at the Hackney Empire. After the reception he got, London E9 became twinned with Nuremburg. Mosley himself was stiff all over by this point, a condition that had spread from his right arm at the time of death, but his wife Diana (one of the Mitford girls) was still at large in Paris. A few years later, I interviewed her younger sister at Chatsworth for Radio Four's arts strand, *Kaleidoscope.* Sharing a sofa with the Duchess of Devonshire, I was relieved she didn't do a double-take and say...

DUCHESS: Good God, you look just like my late brother-in-law!

A striking physical resemblance to the evil one might have been a plus on stage but it was a distinct minus for other gigs on nights off from the play. I couldn't remove the slimy moustache without shaving, then there would be no time to re-grow it for the next performance. So it was that I honoured a booking to warm up a cosy TV sitcom, chatting affably to the studio audience while appearing to be the long-lost twin of Britain's most notorious fascist. The programme in question, *Don't Wait Up*, attracted the type of punters who'd been through the war and were less than happy to be reminded of it. My pitiful attempts to keep the crowd amused between scenes fell on stony faces and the silence only broke when cast members Nigel Havers and Simon Williams were around to rescue me. The director, Harold Snoad, even popped down to the studio floor himself in a bid to save the situation, shooting me a look that seemed to say...

SNOAD'S LOOK: Next time I'll book Martin Boorman.

There is a precise craft to warming up an audience. People like Bill Martin (brother of George Martin, Basil Brush's scriptwriter), Felix Bowness and more recently Jeff Stevenson have made careers of it. Felix (the jockey in *Hi De Hi!*) would hold up a photo of his grandchildren, wait two seconds then declare indignantly...

FELIX: I normally get a round of applause for that.

...and miraculously, the crowd would begin to clap as if Pavlov were conducting an experiment. Bill had a better line in good old sure-fire jokes (or boffers, as they're known). If things went a bit too quiet, he'd hold his nerve, hold the pause, then say casually…

BILL: Still no sign of Glenn Miller then.

You see? A craft. Keep them smiling but don't overshadow the main event. Bob Monkhouse once described the ideal warm-up act as…

BOB M: A good frame-maker for the painter who follows.

Just my luck: I never could do woodwork.

After my 'don't warm up' experience, I compared notes with a couple of friends who were veterans of this particular battleground and was selfishly relieved to find myself in good company. A comedienne and songstress chum had managed to get herself sacked for warming up too well! According to the floor manager, she had got such good audience response that the star said…

STAR: Don't book her again.

I couldn't possibly reveal the star's name but the show was called *Alexei Sayle's Stuff*.

Dick Vosburgh was almost certainly lying to cheer me up but the way he told it…

DICK: Last time I warmed up an audience, three people died of hypothermia.

HECKLER: Get off!

COMIC: Sorry, I don't do requests.

9

BREMNER BUT NO FORTUNE

"Rory Bremner had a gallery of gold-standard impressions but piss-poor material."

Consumed by an overwhelming urge to put money in my account (the urge coming from my bank manager), I forsook the unpaid swamp of the fringe and headed back to the lucrative terraine of telly writing...but matters were not helped due to a false start called Ernest Maxin. In his capacity as producer of Les Dawson's BBC1 show, Ernest had seen fit to reject my material because he thought it was crap (his prerogative) and to deny me the second half of my fee (an outrage!). I mean, rejection one can live with - but how do you live without dosh?

The happy ending to this sorry tale came years later when the BBC brought out a Dawson video and DVD in their *Comedy Greats* series for which I was paid and received a credit, despite the fact that not one word of mine ever passed Les's lips. As I say though, that was far into the future. At the time, I was not just impecunious but skint with it and the only work available was out-of-vision bit parts on TV sitcoms. Thanks to a generous production manager called Andy Smith, I found my way onto the soundtracks of *Sorry!*, *Just Good Friends* and *Only Fools And Horses*. The last of these three has done so well abroad over the decades that it's now earned me more than any of the jobs I've really had to sweat over. And if I get £17.50 whenever it's sold to somewhere like Trinidad and Tobago, I wonder how much David Jason's on. Still, my initial fees were modest so a cash cow had to be found and milked - and in the mid-'80s, cows didn't come much more cashtastic than LWT.

On my first visit to London Weekend, I was struck by the lush extravagance of my surroundings: mirrored ceilings, thick pile carpet, art deco lamps...and that was just the lift.

Now that's an old joke but in this case, it was true.

As the doors parted, there to greet me was Kev, hellbent on poaching all the BBC's talent, starting with himself and moving on to the likes of Kim Fuller, Andrea Solomons, Tony Sarchet the hair-twiddler and, thankfully, me.

We were gathered together to bring jokes to a new series showcasing Chris Barrie (still an impressionist in those pre-Rimmer days), the actress and singer Carla Mendonca and a couple of renegades from the troupe Fundation, Gareth Hale and Norman Pace. The finished product, *Pushing up Daisies*, bore no resemblance to a more recent series of nearly the same name. I felt the title suggested a rather naff sitcom set in a funeral parlour. Of course, what we should have called it was *The Lenny Henry Show*.

Hale and Pace's meteoric rise into cor-blimey-missus territory is all too well documented. Carla is now best-known as an actress but I felt her outstanding gift was her singing voice. One of my happiest moments on the series was when she delivered a Reagan lyric of mine which described him as being...

CARLA:...over the Capitol Hill and just as cosy as Amity- ville.

Chris Barrie was probably very glad of Ronnie's presence on the world stage as it enabled him to show off the best of his impressions - though he also did a cracking Ian Paisley getting arrested outside Stormont Castle.

CHRIS:(PAISLEY)It's all right officer, I'LL COME QUIETLY!!

I'm sure these skills provided Chris with a giant's causeway-size stepping stone to unseen fame on *Spitting Image*, a show I was asked to write for but declined as I couldn't think of sufficiently visual items. Any series like it (and there have been several, from *2DTV* to *Headcases*) requires writing that has the puppets, cartoons or whatever doing things that actors can't do. Actually, there are many things actors can't do, like stop whining about the billing, their fee and the fact they're not playing at the National, but you know what I mean: a giant David Owen beside a miniscule David Steele would never have worked with real people (or actors), any more than the sight gag of Mark Thatcher emerging from a panel in the door of 10 Downing Street labelled 'prat flap'.

The production company called itself Spitting Image from day one but the producer (John Lloyd...again) told me a magnum of champagne would go to whoever came up with the best title for the series. Consequently, many were offered including, notably, 'Rubber News' and 'The Late Latex Show' (both Grant and Naylor's, I think) but as we all know, the firm's name was the one that eventually hit the screens. Dear me, what some folk will do to avoid giving booze away. By the way, if you don't get 'Rubber News', you're not alone: it's the name of a fetishist publication...apparently...so I'm told.

One impressionist who didn't join the Spit rep company till much later on was Rory Bremner. I first met him when we were on the same bill at a comedy night in Earl's Court (isn't every night a comedy night in Earl's Court?). Like Chris Barrie, he had a gallery of gold-standard impressions but piss-poor material. His top gag was about an MP, Cecil Parkinson, who impregnated his mistress then resigned, raising the question...

RORY [AS ROBIN DAY]: Should he have pulled out sooner?

Coincidentally, I'd done the same line myself a year before but the point is this: if that was his best joke, Rory needed a writer.

By far the most suitable candidate in my view was John Langdon who led a double-life as a comedy creator and a guitarist in a Russian-style duo called Bibs and Vanya, complete with cossack costumes and furry hats.

Perhaps I should have set myself up as a computer dating service for writers and turns because, twenty-six years on from introducing John to Rory, I see they're still joined at the comedy hip. At that time, the young Bremner and I were performing together for the late Geoffrey Perkins in a spoof DJ series for London's Capital Radio which sent up pop shows so accurately that the station refused to broadcast it (also in the cast was Ken Morley before he thrilled the nation as *Corrie*'s Reg Holdsworth). Then we met again on Rory's TV debut where I was drafted in as script editor. Now there's a weird job. You're not really one of the writing team but the production staff don't treat you as a grown-up either. The only way to fulfill the post adequately is to be two people, a trick I've never perfected (and neither have I). One of you needs to be in the office, going through the mounds of hilarity the writers have sent in, while the other should monitor what's being changed by the cast in the rehearsal room so you know which writers to apologise to when they don't recognise their own sketches at the recording.

One of them, my dear chum Dick Vosburgh, gave me quite a hard time about this - and probably rightly so. Our friendship survived but this wasn't the only example of Dick becoming caustic if crossed. After a falling-out with Ronnie Barker over a Dr. Spooner sketch on *The Two Ronnies*, the star was sent a one-line note, reading...

DICK: Parker, you're a brick.

...and then there was the theatre director of whom Dick remarked...

DICK: The amount of respect I have for that man could be inserted into the navel of a gnat!

Gems like that are what prompted me later to describe Mr. Vosburgh as 'Dorothy Parker with a beard'.

Most of the Bremner writing team, however, was surprisingly good-natured and philosophical about the various unscheduled rewrites, notably Brighton-based Jeremy Pascall. I was gutted when one of his best lines was cut. It concerned an egocentric and upper-crust TV celeb of the time who had...

JEREMY:...finally got in touch with his inner child. All he needs now is an inner nanny to look after it.

Mind you, Pascall had other fish to fry, being the host of a radio panel game called *You Ain't Heard Nothing Yet*. One of his regular team captains was that doyen of DJs Peter Young, known as much for his wit as his musical knowledge. Because of the nature of PY and Jeremy's faux-combative on-air relationship, it was suggested the show be re-named 'Two Middle-Aged Bearded Men Shouting At Each Other'. Peter told me he once sat down at home with his uncle, listening to an edition of *YAHNY*, after which the uncle enquired...

UNCLE: Tell me Peter, is this a

live programme or is it recorded?

Pete of course replied that the show was live but that his presence at home was pre-recorded.

Meanwhile, back at the new, as yet nameless Rory Bremner show, because the young turk was still unknown to the public, our elder statesman producer and thrusting young blade director decided against including his name in the programme's title (despite an attempt on the young master's part to call it 'The Rory So Far'), so they were open to offers. No magnum of champagne this time: at the Beeb, you'd be lucky to bag a half-bottle of Frascati. Naturally, I suggested *The Lenny Henry Show* but this and all other punts were rejected in favour of one sent in by a Mr. M. Grade of Wood Lane, West London. He decreed that this brand new show should be called *Now...Something Else*, possibly the worst title in the entire history of television. Not only did it sound like a pale and inferior echo of

Monty Python's *And Now for Something Completely Different*, it also caused confusion with another BBC2 show called *Something Else*. Jeremy Hardy remarked to me that if we were going to name the programme after an existing series, we might as well call it *Steptoe and Son*.

Jeremy and I had been in an Edinburgh show together in 1984, his first Fringe (before he got his Fringe First). I warned him how cold Scotland was and urged him to take warm clothes. We had a heatwave that August and he could be seen round the city in a worsted three-piece, cursing me as he mopped the sweat from his brow/armpits/crotch etc.

On TV, he made a weekly cameo appearance as a cardigan-clad work ex-perience boom-mike operator, enabling him to do his stand-up routine without it looking like stand-up. Rory topped and tailed each show with monologues (written largely by Langdon, often typing the gags directly onto the autocue as our star, on-camera, read them for the first time) in which he'd slide effortlessly from Sean Connery to Barry Norman via eccentric figures of fun like Peter Snow and Prince Charles. At no point did he appear as himself, unlike today when much of the time he'll address the camera in his own voice, doubtless prompting the viewing millions to wonder...

VIEWING MILLIONS: Who's that meant to be?

Now...Some Dreadful Title was scarcely the happiest ship in the harbour, mainly because its captain and first mate were all at sea. Before this paragraph turns into *Mutiny On The Bounty*, I'd best explain: our elder statesman producer and thrusting young blade director didn't agree on much and each was determined to get his own way. In the end, neither succeeded as both were scared of certain cast members with far stronger personalities than theirs. Not Rory, though, who was enthusiastically charming to everyone. He'd also go to enormous lengths to let you know how busy he was. It was a case of…

RORY: Give us a bell if you need to chat I'll be in Edinburgh tonight Brighton tomorrow Birmingham on Wednesday then three nights on the Isle of Man.

Not so much a conversation as a gig guide. I'm amazed he stopped short of listing the ticket prices.

The resulting series was a bit of a mish-mash (to use a technical term), rescued from bog-standard sketchland by Rory's impressions, Jeremy's meanderings and the bleakly comic songs of John Dowie, a mordant figure whose gallows outlook was typified by ditties like *I'm Here To Entertain You With Songs About Depression* (in which he rhymed 'humour' with 'tumour'), *I'm Glad That We Broke Up, Aren't You?* and my personal favourite, *I Don't Want To Be Your Amputee.*

Some of the sketches did achieve distinction, usually when they hinged on a Bremner impersonation and especially if he was teamed with cast member Steve Steen, himself no slouch as a mimic. Memorably, they lampooned the Mel and Griff head-to-head format in a sharp parody by Ian Brown and exhibited a new twist on James Bond by having Connery (Steve) and Moore (Rory) in wheelchairs in an old folks' home where they squabbled over which of them was closer to Ian Fleming's idea of 007.

MOORE: He said he wanted an English actor to play Bond and you're not English.

CONNERY: And you're not an actor.

As we broke up at the end of series one, the young Scot was on stardom fast-track. In time, Michael Grade's dreadful title was duly ditched in favour of *Rory Bremner* (that's more like it) and the thrusting young blade director wrested the tiller of command from the elder statesman producer who went back to his *Little and Large* duties with, I suspect, a sense of relief. I was equally relieved to be relieved of my script-editing post by the late John Langdon (he's still alive, he's just always late). After months of trying to calm troubled waters, I was starting to run out of oil. John's unflappable nature made him a far more suitable mediator, coupled with the fact that by the time he turned up, everyone had forgotten what the row was about in the first place.

Q: After a few pints, what do comics find hard to do?

A: Stand up.

10

A TURKEY IN CYPRUS

"Peter Sellers decided his character's name was putting a curse on the project and insisted he should be called Dick Scratcher."

When I met Gary Oldman again in the late 1990s, he was twenty years and two wives older. His devoted mother, Kay, had thoughtfully invited me to a preview of her lad's directorial debut, *Nil by Mouth* where I met the surprisingly short (though unsurprisingly stout) Ray Winstone and stood next to Pete Townshend in the gents. Oh, the glamour of showbiz. Gary's sister Maureen was there, as well as in the film. I remembered her from our drama school days when she'd scoffed at acting, saying it wasn't real work. She's in *Eastenders* now.

Gary's warts-and-all cinematic portrait of South London having been unleashed on the public, he returned to the even more savage environs of California (have you seen those toupees? Terrifying!) but was back in the UK soon after to make *Lost in Space* or as it really was, 'Lost In Shepperton'. I went to see him on the set and he was eager for me to meet a director chum of his to discuss writing a screenplay about Peter Sellers. This director was a Hungarian émigré called Peter Medak who had worked with the ex-Goon on *Ghost in the Noonday Sun*, a 1973 disaster movie. It wasn't meant to be a disaster; it just was.

Gary is blessed with a great deal more humour than his saturnine screen roles would have you believe. One of his earliest TV appearances had been in *The Borgias* for BBC2 where he was struck by the hilarious sight of fifteenth-century cardinals reading *The Sun* between takes. When it came to portraying a comic villain in the Luc Besson movie *The Fifth Element*, Gary relished the chance to camp it up, especially in the scenes where he was partnered by a Bristolian rapper with no acting ability whatsoever (great casting, eh?). Besson cleverly 'forgot' to alert the rapper to an impending explosion sequence as he knew this was the only way he'd get the boy to give a reaction of genuine shock. It worked - and the film's worth watching for that nanosecond alone.

Given his capacity for mirth, Gary was convinced there was more fun to be had in a film about the making of the Sellers picture than there ever had been in the piece itself. I certainly hoped so for Peter Medak's sake. After *GITNS*, he didn't work for nearly five years despite having a CV that boasted *A Day In The Death Of Joe Egg* by Peter Nichols and *The Ruling Class*, penned by Peter Barnes. Let me know if this chapter gets a bit Peter-heavy.

Medak was charming and tremendously helpful, not just in providing me with square miles of background on the behind-the-scenes catastrophes but also in guiding my unsteady (and previously untried) cinema screenwriter's hand.

In a somewhat oversized nutshell, the reason *GITNS* made most lead balloons look featherlight was the erratic behaviour of its star. Sellers it was who convinced Medak that a wacky pirate romp was just what the early '70s movie scene was lacking. This was true…but there was a good reason for this: pirate romps are rarely that wacky, as Graham Chapman and Marty Feldman discovered a decade later with *Yellowbeard* (though poor Feldman never lived to see the result).

Another problem with *GITNS* was the script. It stank and Medak knew it: they were shooting in Cyprus and he could smell it from London. But getting Sellers to sit down and work on rewrites proved impossible as the leading man was too busy calling press conferences announcing his engagement to a close relative of Judy Garland. One wag remarked that if the wedding had gone ahead, there'd have been three fruitcakes at the reception.

On arrival in Kyrenia, the beautiful Cypriot port where cast and crew were to be based, a further problem arose when the ship earmarked for shooting crashed into the quayside, courtesy of a drunken captain, putting the schedule back by a fortnight. While they mended the holes in the boat, Medak thought he'd make good use of this down-time by mending the holes in the script. However, that proved impossible as his leading man (who needed to be there for this process) was too busy flying back to Blighty for drinkies with a close relative of the Queen.

Later, once shooting was finally under way, Sellers suddenly decided his character's name was putting a curse on the project. Having cast himself as Dick Scratch, he then discovered that Scratch is an old name for the devil and insisted the character should become Dick Scratcher. Oh well, at least he did one rewrite. Other 'improvements' had to be postponed as he was too busy fighting with co-star Tony Franciosa, turning on

Medak himself and firing Larry Pizer, the cameraman that he'd hired in the first place.

After interviewing Peter Medak over a few days, I was beginning to see why I'd never heard of *Ghost in the Noonday Sun* at the time of its release: it went straight to video, which was tricky as video hadn't been invented yet.

But having appeared throughout the early '70s in a string of stinkers of which *GITNS* was the latest and by far the stinkiest, Sellers regained popularity soon afterwards, principally because cinema audiences saw him once more in the Inspector Clouseau garb and demand grew for a second outbreak of Pink Panther films. He'd worn the trademark hat and coat in a cigarette commercial shot on Cyprus (by Medak) during one of the few breaks in filming that didn't involve a trip back home for cocktails with royalty.

If you ever get the chance to see this curious little ad, you'll notice that of the three actors in it, only James

Villiers actually handles the fag packet. This is because Sellers was by then President of the Anti-Smoking League and the other participant (one Spike Milligan) objected to Benson & Hedges on pollution grounds. Neither would be filmed touching the product but were happy to be seen in the ad and take the money for it (though Milligan's get-out clause was that he would donate his fee to Friends of the Earth). If Villiers had objected too, Medak would have had to employ a stunt 'hand double' or one of those poles for opening skylights. But here's how the action goes:-

SCENE: A SMALL MOTOR BOAT PULLS UP AT THE QUAYSIDE WHERE A GOLD VAULT HAPPENS TO BE SITUATED. JACQUES LOUSSIER-STYLE PIANO PLAYS THROUGHOUT.

THREE CROOKS (SELLERS, VILLIERS & MILLIGAN) DISEMBARK AND POINT POINTEDLY AT THE VAULT WHERE GOLD IS VISIBLE THROUGH THE IRON BARS. SELLERS HEADS STRAIGHT FOR THE BARS BUT IS RESTRAINED BY MILLIGAN WHO POINTS, SILENT COMEDY-STYLE, AT

A BURGLAR ALARM. THEY SEARCH
THEIR POCKETS FOR SOMETHING
TO DISABLE IT AND VILLIERS
PRODUCES A GOLD B&H PACK.
SELLERS & MILLIGAN LOOK ON
AND POINT AS VILLIERS WEDGES
PACKET BETWEEN ALARM'S HAMMER
AND BELL. SELLERS THROWS
VAULT DOOR OPEN, BEGINS
HELPING HIMSELF TO GOLD.
MILLIGAN STORES SO MANY BARS
IN HIS POCKETS THAT HE CAN
BARELY MOVE. THEY MAKE TO
LEAVE BUT SELLERS POINTS TO
B&H PACKET WHICH VILLIERS
REMOVES, CAUSING ALARM TO
RING.
SELLERS & VILLIERS LEAP INTO
BOAT BUT ARE HELD UP BY
MILLIGAN WHO STRUGGLES TO
QUAYSIDE EDGE AND THROWS
HIMSELF OFF. THE WEIGHT OF
THE GOLD CAUSES HIM TO CRASH
THROUGH THE BOAT.

Meantime, back at the screenplay about
the making of the movie, roughly a
year after being offered the project by
Gary, I emerged with a script entitled
In the Mood (both the title of the Glenn

Miller tune played at Sellers's funeral and a neatish summing-up of what the star had to be in order to work). Messrs Oldman and Medak both liked it and gave me invaluable pointers as to how it could be improved. Sellers, long dead, was in no position to comment. However, in the best Hollywood tradition, the film never got made. We came close to a deal with Intermedia but HBO already had *The Life and Death of Peter Sellers* on their books (an excellent piece of writing) and that cinema screen wasn't big enough for the both of them. Knew I should have done *The Harry Secombe Story* instead.

Or maybe *The Story of Spike*. TAPS Milligan (Terence Alan Patrick Sean) was the only Goon I met and my favourite by far, partly because he wrote most of the scripts. But meeting your comedy heroes isn't always a good thing. Short of trotting out the hoary old chestnut…

ME: I've always admired your work.

…what in the name of Bob Todd do

you say to them? I once passed the highly gifted playwright Alan Plater in a BBC corridor without a word because all I could think of was...

ME: I've always admired your work.

...and I didn't dare subject him to that. Another time, having just been introduced to each other at a party then left to get on with it, Victoria Wood and I had a conversation that went...

ME:

VICTORIA:

ME:

VICTORIA:

[LONG DEATHLY PAUSE]

ME:

VICTORIA:

…until neither of us could stand it any more and we retreated to opposite corners.

With Spike, there was at the very least a requirement to say something as I'd been booked to interview him for one of Cathay Pacific's inflight audio channels. Producer Nick Carpenter thought I'd be the ideal replacement for the proposed interviewer, a celebrity sports presenter who had turned the prospect down flat with the words…

CELEBRITY SPORTS PRESENTER: I'm not interviewing him. He's fucking mad!

Well, you could see his point. Milligan was notorious for host-baiting. On Kenny Everett's Capital Radio breakfast show, Spike consistently answered all questions with either a…

SPIKE: Yes.

…or a…

SPIKE: No.

...even when the question didn't warrant a 'yes' or 'no' response. And all because the driver had arrived an hour early and woken him up; hardly Kenny's fault. On a different occasion at the same station, my dear friend Peter Young, cigarette in hand, went down to greet Spike in reception. The great Goon's first words to him were...

SPIKE: If you don't put that out now, I'm leaving.

Pete did - and mercifully, Spike didn't...but it had been a close thing. Once he'd got Milligan into the studio and the live interview began, PY's heart sank when Spike was asked an obviously pre-scripted question by the guest presenter (a well-known singer/songwriter)...

PRESENTER: Spike, what has been your most embarrassing moment?

...and the reply was...

SPIKE: This is it!

Armed with all this daunting information, I resisted the urge to light up (not hard as I've never smoked and couldn't even get it right when required to do so on stage), resolved not to mention embarrassing moments, prayed to the god of courtesy cars that the driver hadn't woken Spike (mid-afternoon, so unlikely yet possible) and on his arrival, tried not to wince when the well-meaning engineer (another Bob and another life-long Milligan fan) noticed the faintness of Spike's voice and suggested he spoke directly into the microphone. He did.

SPIKE: I'm not a cretin, you know.

...were the words he chose. Oh dear. But I was lucky. After a fairly ramshackle start, he thawed out a bit though I sensed he still didn't trust me. Then I asked...

ME: Spike, could you put your headphones on? There's a record I'd like to play you.

He did so, muttering...

SPIKE: I expect this'll be The Ying-Tong Song.

He expected wrong. Instantly, his face began to shine as he heard the 1972 single, *Girl on a Pony* which he'd written and recorded; a sentimental ghost story without a joke in it.

SPIKE: I haven't heard this since we did it!

Clearly a favourite - and for some reason, he didn't own a copy. Producer Nick promised to provide him with one and after that, he couldn't do enough for us. I knew we'd won him round when the interview ended thus:-

ME: Spike Milligan, thank you.

SPIKE [HAND OUTSTRETCHED]: That'll be a pound.

Of course, among many other things, I asked him about *Ghost in the Noonday Sun* and he confirmed it had been a disaster due to Peter Sellers's flakiness. There was praise, though, for Peter Medak and I knew the admiration was mutual.

In the end, I was more disappointed for Medak than myself at *In The Mood*'s failure to storm the multiplexes. It might have given the dear old Hungarian some form of 'closure' (whatever that is). For me, yes, the cash would have been welcome but in the film world you only cop the big bucks if your project makes it to day one of principal photography - and that's one big 'if'. Even then, many scribes come and go on a picture and are regarded by the producers as highly expendable. They certainly have very little influence and almost no power. Ian McEwan once joked about the starlet who was so naïve that she tried furthering her career by shagging a writer.

McEwan's not known for witty one-liners and he's not particularly renowned for his screenplays but I retain a soft spot for his early-'80s effort, *The Ploughman's Lunch*, partly because at one degree of separation, it's the closest I've ever come to cinematic immortality.

Everyone of my generation had a Ford Anglia or had an uncle or a cousin or a milkman who owned one. Mine was bought in the late 70s, way past the model's crush-by date, but just in time for the retro-chic era. Vivian of *The Young Ones* crashed his Ford spectacularly in the show's final episode and mine was to achieve brief stardom in the aforementioned movie.

There's a scene, late in the film, where Jonathan Pryce emerges from the foyer of BBC Broadcasting House, bound for Regent Street. He was shot (with a camera, not a gun) from the top step of All Souls' Church, Langham Place and in those days you could park just outside. What the viewer saw was a commanding frontal image of my white 105E saloon, its registration number fully displayed in the foreground, while poor Jonathan was milling about somewhere towards the rear of the shot, fighting the car for screen space - and losing.

1st COMIC: Don't you hate it when people say, 'Go on, do something funny'?

2nd COMIC: Yes, especially when I'm on stage.

11

TWO BOB BIT

"Bob was consistently kind, almost paternal, towards me, regarding me as a loveable goof."

I didn't think I'd like Bob Monkhouse. His Cheshire Cat image (the butt of jokes in *Beyond Our Ken* as far back as 1961), coupled with his reputation among disgruntled writers as 'the thief of bad gags' didn't auger well. Then in 1999, something happened that changed my mind: I met him.

This was the decade when Bill Clinton discovered the harmful effects of cigars, when human cloning became a reality with the advent of Ant and Dec...and when Monkhouse reclaimed his comedian status after decades of being dismissed as a smarmy game-show host.

I'd been asked to write a four-part radio series on Bob Hope who, amazingly, was still alive, three years younger than the century and in slightly better nick. A star name was needed to present the programmes and the most likely candidate was Jonathan Ross. Why? Well, he hadn't been on the air for hours.

Now don't get me wrong: Ross is pleasant enough (as I'd discovered when appearing on his show to plug one of mine). My only reservation with him is that, when you strip away all the hype, I really don't think he's that good. This is highly subjective, of course, but for me it's the king's new clothes - or in this case, Jean-Paul Gaultier's new clothes - so when he appeared atop the Bob Hope list of probable presenters, I took a sudden interest in the names lower down.

And there, bubbling under, was Bob Monkhouse whose credits, I vaguely recalled, included a spell as one of Hope's cue-card inscribers in the '50s. If I'd got this right, it struck me as a pretty good reason for choosing him to host the series (not that it was up to me. If you think writers have any power, I refer you to the Ian McEwan anecdote on page 187).

Granted, as a writer, you can sometimes influence casting (if you make the producer think it was their idea) but really the final decision does rest with said producer. This is why it's easy to spot a show that's been produced by a woman I'll call Zena Tiles: not so much her trademark production style or anything to do with the type of programme, more the fact that her actor boyfriend will be in it. Some casting remains inexplicable to medical science. One producer I worked with seemed to be in love with the idea of using a popular poet from East Anglia in comedy sketches with the result that one of mine couldn't even be rescued by the presence of the mighty Paula Wilcox and Graeme Garden. It was a three-hander and the third hand (the popular poet) had forgotten to bring any acting talent.

Meantime, back at *The Bob Hope Story*, consulting whatever research material existed pre-Google (and believe it or not, there was some), I found that Bob M had indeed sought out Bob H backstage at London's Prince of Wales Theatre in 1953, thanks to an introduction from the actor Jerry Desmonde (best known as Norman Wisdom's straight man) and presented the visiting comic with a string of gags, some of which duly received the magic Hope tick in the margin. It was a big thrill for the 24-year-old Monkhouse, so much so that money wasn't mentioned by either party. Of course, Hope did pay his regular script team but, according to Dick Vosburgh who worked for him in the '60s, this involved a ritual where the great man would stand at the top of a staircase and let go of a batch of cheques which then floated down to the writers below; no truth in the rumour that this only occurred on Maundy Thursday.

Dick didn't tell that one on-air but he did give us an interview recalling Hope's consternation backstage at the London Palladium when the compere, Tommy Trinder, came on at rehearsal and read half of Hope's act off the cue cards strategically placed round the auditorium.

HOPE: He's not going to do that on the night, is he?!

Dick assured him this was just fun-loving Tommy having a giggle but Hope's reaction shows just how much he relied on his board members...so called because they had to write their jokes on boards. For his British dates, Bob Hope would usually recruit Monkhouse and his writing partner, Denis Goodwin, often supervising them personally in his hotel suite. Once, when Monkhouse excused himself and repaired to the bathroom, he'd just got settled when there was a knock on the door and an American voice shouted...

HOPE: There's paper in there. Keep writing!

With all this in mind, it struck me that Bob M was the obvious choice to present *The Bob Hope Story* - and unbelievably, the BBC actually agreed!

Sorry, Jonathan: I'm sure your day will come when they need someone for *The Andrew Sachs Story*.

I always enjoyed making programmes about American artists, largely because they often involved a trip to…America. For *The Bob Hope Story*, we met and interviewed Phyllis Diller (his sometime movie co-star) and business really did turn into pleasure when I was given access to my long-time comedy hero, Stan Freberg. This was for a series about the history of the Capitol record label for which Stan had recorded many masterpieces including *The Banana Boat Song* (Harry Belafonte never forgave him) and his gangster spoof *St. George and the Dragonet* where Jack Webb, star of the real *Dragnet*, was so keen that the music should sound right that he lent Freberg the entire orchestra.

Mel Torme was among the musical legends I encountered on an earlier BBC-funded jaunt (i.e. you paid for it) to the States…and there is a comedy connection here. Mel's third wife was

Janette Scott, daughter of the formidable Thora Hird. Before becoming the cuddly *Songs of Praise* national treasure of her final years, Thora had made a steady living as a battleaxe, notably in the film *A Kind of Loving* and alongside Freddie Frinton in the TV sitcom *Meet the Wife*. Now, the fact that she was this revered crooner's ma-in-law conjures an image of the great Torme storming the room at Caesar's Palace, getting home at 3am, undoing his bow-tie and loosening his cummerbund only to be berated by a figure in curlers, brandishing a rolling-pin and barking…

THORA: And what time of night do you call this, young man? My daughter's been sitting here, eating her heart out!

One sobering footnote: my first flight to New York at Auntie's behest was on Pan Am 103 and the journey occurred a fortnight before the Lockerbie crash. Not many laughs there. But arriving on the twenty-first floor of the Rockefeller Centre, I was surprised to be greeted by the widow of a British comedy legend.

FREDDIE: Hallo darling, my name's Freddie Hancock. Now let's get you sorted out with some contacts.

[RIFFLES THROUGH HER ADDRESS BOOK.]

Cyril Stapleton? No, he's dead. John Le Mesurier? He's dead. I wish his fucking wife was!

If that reference baffles you, any one of the many Hancock biographies will make it crystal clear.

People are often surprised by the roster of big names who are only too happy to turn out on the humble wireless, despite the fees being so small as to be undetectable to the human bank manager (if that's not an oxymoron). To return to Bob Monkhouse, he was a shining example of this. With his TV and stage diaries full to bursting, he didn't need the faceless medium to boost his profile or his income. But he was a vocational entertainer. Fame for its own sake didn't interest him: he liked it for the increased opportunities it brought him to work as a comic - and that, as he said on his final *Parkinson* appearance...

BOB M:...is what I'm for.

He certainly didn't need guest spots on shows like mine (*Dr Sin's Laughter Zone* on the fledgling digital station, Oneword Radio) but it gave him the chance to write new stuff (yes, Monkhouse wrote for me as well as the other way round) and perform with new talents like Lynsey Frost, Jeff Downs and Lindley Gooden - and slightly older ones like me. In short, he lapped it up.

And he wasn't the only one. Over the decades, I've found myself writing for - and sharing sound studios with - Richard 'Stinker' Murdoch, Joan Sims, Geoffrey Palmer (whose stomach wouldn't shut up), Alan Cumming, David Suchet, Leslie Phillips (who was quite prepared to say...

...even though he hated doing it), Eleanor Bron, Brenda Blethyn, Lee Hurst (brilliantly funny in the office as well as on air), Joanna Lumley, Dick Emery (who arrived with two women whom I took to be his wife and daughter; but the 'wife' was his manager and the 'daughter' was his wife), Terry-Thomas (though sadly he was so ill by then that his projected radio comeback never made it to air), Arthur English (famous as a comedy spiv long before Private Walker) and, bless my soul, Rory McGrath (was he stalking me?).

Oh yes, and Tim Brooke-Taylor. Tim's was the first name I heard on the first radio comedy programme I discovered for myself (*I'm Sorry, I'll Read That Again* always listed its cast alphabetically) and as a kid, I would try listening to it under the bedclothes. This became easier when my mum bought me a radio.

Tim was pleased when I managed to write a short series for him in an even shorter space of time and on discovering I didn't have an agent, he generously rewarded me by recommending his. Poor Jill Foster. Despite her best efforts over subsequent years to groom me for TV sitcom success, I remained a sad disappointment, preferring to focus on just about anything that lacked commercial viability. How her heart must have sunk when I rang with news like…

```
ME    (PHONE    QUALITY):    Jill,
guess what?  I'm co-writing a
spoof of Twelve Angry Men to
go  out  on  Radio  Two  after
midnight!
```

No exaggeration, I'm afraid. *Twelve Grumpy Men* (how <u>did</u> we think of them?) was indeed heard by the handful of listeners still conscious in the wee small hours and starred wee small Maurice Denham as a batty judge with me as his prissy clerk of the court. Also in the cast was John Langdon, the other half of the writing team. Collaboration's a four-letter word to me but only because I've always been rubbish at it…oh, and because I can't spell. Traditionally, a writing pair subdivides into the sitter-at-the-keyboard and the pacer-on-the-floorboards. The former organises the creative chaos pouring out of the latter. With John, who is anatomically conjoined with his laptop, I'd pace. But he's also a great one for creative chaos so I'd start to wonder why I was there at all. There were probably times when he wondered that. Still, having an actor in mind to write for doesn't half help and we could just hear the judge's preposterous pronouncements coming out of Maurice Denham's mouth. Good job he said yes.

Maurice was a true comedy veteran, having made a name for himself in the 1940s sitcom *Much Binding in the Marsh*. The name he made was Dudley Davenport and in those catchphrase-heavy days, his was…

DUDLEY: Oh I am a fool!

Unlike Dudley, the actor playing him was no fool; Maurice was one wily old fox, adopting the guise of an elderly buffer but never missing a trick. Come the recording date for *Twelve Grumpy Men*, as Maurice and I entered the BBC lift that was to take us to our studio in the sub-lower-sub-sub-basement (one floor above Australia), he made an observation you don't hear from many thesps:-

MAURICE: I installed these lifts, you know.

I laughed, taking this to be merry banter...but later discovered that before his acting career, Maurice Denham had indeed been a lift engineer with a firm called Otis Waygood (whom I'd always thought was a soul singer).

BBC lifts could tell many tales if only they could say something other than...

LIFT: Eighth floor: canteen.

...etc. Chris Morris of *Brass Eye* and *Four Lions* fame told me he was once alone in the front lift at Broadcasting

House and found himself breaking wind in a fairly potent manner just as the doors opened at the third floor and Sir Robin Day stepped in. Before the full might of Chris's expulsion hit the air, Sir Robin pressed the button for the eighth-floor canteen but within seconds, he revised his decision and got out on the fourth. Not a word was spoken in this mini-elevator-drama but it's odd to think that such a cutting-edge comic as Chris Morris took part in a real-life incident that resembled a Benny Hill sketch.

I never met Benny Hill properly but I did once see him walk down a BBC corridor beside a production secretary and couldn't work out why he wasn't persuing her at high speed to the tune of *Yakety Sax*. Then I remembered this was real life. From that day forward, I resolved to try and tell the difference.

Despite being among the first comedians I ever saw on TV, hosting *Sunday Night at the London Palladium*, Jimmy Tarbuck was only in my real-life field of vision for just over a minute. A radio producer rang up in a panic (which suited him), asking if I would visit Tarby (who lives near me but even nearer a golf course), armed with my mini-disc recorder and get him to say two words: Denis Norden. To explain, our chirpy Scouser had recently taped the narration for a documentary featuring a Norden clip but had failed to identify the great man. Thus it fell to me to shove a microphone up Tarby's nose in a bid to immortalise that missing name. Duly, I arrived, was admitted, he finished the phone call he'd been making, we shook hands, he said...

TARBY: Denis Norden.

...about half a dozen times with various inflections, we shook hands again and I left, pondering the fact that we'd have spent even less time together if he'd been called upon to say 'Frank Muir'.

My meeting with Roy Castle was less rushed but just as dramatic. Minutes before we met, he'd refused to shake the hand of Margaret Thatcher at a Dorchester Hotel function, due to her husband's business links with the tobacco industry. Roy had long been a victim of passive smoking (mostly contracted when playing trumpet in jazz dives) and was soon to die because of it. Virtually his first words to me were…

ROY: You'll see it in all the papers tomorrow: 'Tragic Roy Snubs Maggie'.

And he was right, I did.

More often than not, radio comedies were recorded in front of a live(ish) audience, predominantly consisting of pensioners, at the aforementioned Paris studio in Lower Regent Street. Coach parties would attend, usually from somewhere like the Harrow Widows' Club and these old dears would cackle at just about anything provided the comic on stage rolled up his trouserleg when saying it. The worst cackler was called Hetty who was at least 106 and whose trademark braying featured in more shows than most comedians. They were fiendish autograph collectors too, worse than teenage fans with pop stars. One even approached me once, asking…

OLD DEAR: Do I need your autograph?

I assured her that she needed few things less.

Just occasionally, the powers-that-Beeb allowed us out to play in slightly more rarified territory and one April fool night, there I was on stage at the Arts Theatre in Great Newport Street, introducing Vivian Stanshall of Bonzo Dog Doodah Band fame (somewhat oversauced and crippled with nerves). He'd chosen to wear a floor-length monk's habit (borrowed from a floor-length monk) and ill-fitting sandals, then danced near the foot of the stage and nearly fell off. Backstage later, I could see how terrified he'd been as he told me…

VIV: I didn't see what you were doing out there, man. I was too busy shitting myself.

After that, I was quite glad to get back to the Paris. At least it had a sensibly priced tea bar, proving that while there's no such thing as a free lunch, there is such a thing as a cheap one. Well, there was then anyway. This was in the days of student demonstrations against South African apartheid and one Sunday, having nothing more lucrative to do, I popped in just as a heavily-attended rally swept past the main door. Inside, actors were gathered together for a show that was to star Frank Thornton, already famous as the irascible Captain Peacock of Grace Brothers fame in *Are You Being Served?* No sign of him in the building though, and time was getting on.

Eventually, a flustered and blustery figure in a beige mackintosh fell among us, bellowing…

FRANK: Bloody students! Took me half an hour to cross the road!!

One of the supporting cast, Jon Glover, kindly tried to introduce me to

Captain P...I mean Frank Thornton. Mistake. He looked me up and down with undisguised contempt, then snarled...

FRANK: You're not a bloody student, are you?!

There was no answer to that - or none that he wanted to hear. As the celebrity curmudgeon swept past me to the sensibly priced tea bar, I finished my lunch and left, wishing Jon the best of luck.

Yet sometimes, treating the BBC as a media drop-in centre paid off, like the day a producer with a knitted brow (hand-knitted, of course) approached me and said...

PRODUCER: You're not going anywhere.

At first, I thought he was commenting on my career but it soon emerged that Harry Enfield, due to appear in that night's masterpiece, couldn't make it. Not a student demo this time but a double-booking. So it was that I took the big E's place, thanks to a combo of sheer talent and happening to be in the building at the time (though, I suspect, one rather more than the other). I was doubly lucky in that the scenes written with Harry in mind were a good deal funnier that the rest of the script, which was dire. Double-booking, my foreskin! I think he got a better offer elsewhere and ducked out.

Even when the script you're handed isn't exactly comedy gold, you can forgive a lot if the writers are pleasant. In the case of the above, they certainly were - but that's by no means a given. Take the post-war actor Peter Coke. A successful playwright in the days of weekly rep, Coke got lucky when he landed the part of suave detective Paul Temple on BBC radio. He then got unlucky on meeting Temple's creator, Francis Durbridge, whose ice-breaker was...

DURBRIDGE: Now look, I know you're a writer but you needn't think of altering one scintilla of my script.

What a welcome - and how very different from my own experience on being cast in *Molesworth*, the adventures of St. Custard's worst pupil in adult life by Simon Brett. As Grabber, Molesworth's boss, I had a line which didn't sound quite right and I asked Simon if I could change it. Far from doing a Durbridge on me, he couldn't have been more accommodating. By way of a bonus, I got to work with the great Willie Rushton who, when required to do a song as Molesworth, announced to the room…

WILLIE: I shall be singing in the key of H.

Willie had been the first person to play the eighteenth-century rogue Squire Haggard on TV - and decades later, I became the first Squire on stage. Again, I politely requested one or two script changes (being what theatre buffs call an awkward bastard) and merciful heaven, my 'rewrites' got the Green light. I spell 'Green' with a capital G as the author in question was the splendid Michael Green (justly venerated for *The Art of Coarse Acting*). Now in his 80s, Michael still takes a passionate interest in productions of his own work but never in a proprietorial way.

These last few tales serve to illustrate that the writer/performer relationship needn't be an adversarial one. I think my 150 years as a script bunny taught me not to be cavalier when delivering words and phrasings that another writer might have sweated over for whole minutes. And hopefully, I was never snotty with actors and presenters who wanted to change <u>my</u> words and phrasings. It's no coincidence therefore, that I'm alive and Francis Durbridge is dead. That's what happens when you're rude.

As an all-rounder himself, Bob Monkhouse appreciated this etiquette and only ever made constructive suggestions (to me, at any rate). After our joint effort on Bob Hope, we 'traded up' to Radio Four for a one-off *Archive Hour* where I did a sort of *This Is Your*

Life on him, visiting his home (Claridges!) near Leighton Buzzard along with my producer Julian Mayers who had unearthed little surprises from the BBC's Written Archive like the legendary comedy producer Dennis Main Wilson's report on the young Monkhouse's Corporation audition in 1947. Bob had never seen this before and was thrilled (just as well Dennis liked him).

Throughout our various collaborations, Bob was consistently kind, almost paternal, towards me, regarding me as…

BOB M: A loveable goof.

…and was only less than cordial on two occasions. Once, when I arrived behind time with a sketch (a cardinal sin in this business), he greeted me coolly with the question…

BOB M: Are you the new Godfrey Harrison?

I replied that I sincerely hoped not. The old Godfrey Harrison, a writer in the '50s, worked so slowly that his scripts weren't ready till the '60s, by which time the studio audience had gone home. Or died. Or both.

The other awkward moment came when I referred unkindly to a toupee-wearing radio producer so keen to persuade the world he wasn't bald that he had three wigs, each telling a different tale.

WIG A: I'll need a haircut soon.

WIG B: I really do need a haircut.

WIG C: I've just had a haircut.

I mused on what would happen if he got the sequence wrong...to icy silence from the Monkhouse corner. Only years after Bob's death did I glean from some TV documentary that he too was a rugged man (i.e. wore a rug). Who knew?! Like Eric Morecambe, I couldn't see the join.

It didn't matter, though: we stayed friends and collaborated on a short series called *The Oscars: 70 Odd Years* which, although a documentary, still found room for laughs. We kicked off our recording session with the Monkhouse Oscar acceptance speech.

BOB M: I'd like to thank my mother for letting me out tonight, my personal dresser who used to be a tall boy, the man who designed my trailer (and his guide dog), my image consultant (I remember when we used to call them mirrors), my best boy, my worst boy, my creative consultant, my even more creative accountant, my executive cloakroom producer and my agent. Well, ten per cent of him anyway.

He was on his usual chirpy form that day, charming the studio staff and putting everyone at ease. None of them suspected anything was wrong and he delivered the above flawlessly...five minutes after taking me to one side in the green room and calmly telling me his doctor had just given him two years to live.

ME: How do you feel about that?

BOB M: Well, it certainly concentrates the mind.

SCRIPTERS ARE DOING IT FOR THEMSELVES

"The gag trade was becoming a thing of the past."

Bob Monkhouse's death just after Christmas 2003 really did signal the end of an era...and not just for him. When it became clear that he was too ill to work, his *Monkhouse Archive* comedy clip series on Radio Two was shelved in favour of a thing called *Wax On*... which was so self-indulgent that it should have been called 'Whacks Off'. I'm allowed to say this as I worked on it.

The gag trade as I knew it was becoming a thing of the past. Most comedians do their own material now, making them the humour equivalent of the singer/songwriter (though of course, few of them are as funny as Dido).

I lie for comic effect. There are some brilliant 'turns' around but dazzlers such as Milton Jones, Peter Kay, Harry Hill, Shappi Khorsandi, Lee Mack and my local neighbourhood stand-up Tim Vine don't need the likes of me to make them even funnier.

So, never being one to set a trend when I can follow everyone else's, I've written increasingly for myself in recent years. Of course, it doesn't pay so well and there's little prospect of another BAFTA award but the hours are great and the boss is incredibly easy to work with. Someone else who's easy to work with is the TV director Tom Poole, my collaborator and the creator of Scotland Yard's most hapless detectives, DI Flint and DS Bone. I've played Flint on stage and radio and there's even talk of television (but then, there's always talk of television…). Oh yes, and I mustn't forget the books: *Ready Steady Crook* and *Simply Dead* are eminently available (only three million copies have been pulped worldwide). A shameless plug can be found on the next few pages and a taster can be found right here:-

FLINT: London - capital of crime!

BONE: Sir, I think you'll find it's the capital of England.

FLINT: Shut up, Bone. London - epicentre of odious act-ivity.

BONE: That sounds nice, sir.

FLINT: It is not nice. Odious activities are what criminals engage in.

BONE: Crikey! You wouldn't think they'd have time for that, what with all the crime they get up to as well.

FLINT: Bone, shut up! London - home to the very dregs of

humanity.

BONE: You live in London, don't you sir?

FLINT: Well if it comes to that, so do you!

BONE: Ah but I'm only on attachment, see, from the Llandudno constabulary.

FLINT: Yes - a fact they seem to have conveniently overlooked these last six years. Now where was I? London: place where…bad things happen. Against this backdrop of metropolitan vice stands one bulwark of truth and decency: Scotland Yard.

BONE: But sir, just the other day you said the Yard was a toilet bowl full of corrupted drunken half-wits.

FLINT: Bone, what I tell you in the back of the squad car and what we tell the public are two different things! Scotland Yard, wherein lies the infamous Black Museum, housing the relics of the darkest endeavours of the criminal mind.

BONE: Nice touch, sir. Lovely language.

FLINT: Come with me, Detective Inspector Duncan Flint…

BONE: And me, Detective Sergeant Brian Bone, on attachment from Llandudno…

FLINT: As I reveal…

BONE: As we reveal…

FLINT: The secrets of the black museum.

BONE: The secrets of the black museum.

FLINT: Bone.

BONE: Sir?

FLINT: Fuck off and write your own book.

And finally, having written my own book, I'll fuck off too with this modest farewell...

ME: It's funnay...and it is me.

FURTHER READING

THE ENCYCLOPAEDIA OF CLASSIC SATURDAY NIGHT TELLY

Jack Kibble-White & Steve Williams

Allison & Busby, 2007.

At once sassy and comprehensive, this takes in every big show of telly's big night, from the crime series *Dixon of Dock Green* to the just plain criminal *X Factor*.

THE RADIO TIMES GUIDE TO TV COMEDY

Mark Lewisohn

BBC, 1998, 2003.

An exhaustive review of every comedy show to have hit British screens…and *Beggar My Neighbour*.

PRIME MINISTER, YOU WANTED TO SEE ME: A HISTORY OF WEEK ENDING

Ian Greaves & Justin Lewis

Kaleidoscope, 2008.

An exhausting review of every episode ever transmitted, complete with the inside leg measurements, dental records and GCSE results of the additional material writers.

ALL IN THE BEST POSSIBLE TASTE: GROWING UP WATCHING TELLY IN THE 1980S

Tom Bromley

Simon & Schuster, 2010

Memories of the decade which began with just three channels and a midnight closedown. Those were the days.

THE GAG TRADE

Bob Sinfield

Doctor Sin UK, 2011

Unquestionably the best book about TV and radio comedy ever written. What's particularly striking is the author's modesty.

BOB'S TV CV

Some of the author's projects you might have missed…as for some reason, they were never made.

WHOSE LINO IS IT ANYWAY?

Improvised floor show.

RANDALL & HOPKIRK (DISEASED)

A private eye solves cases, helped by his partner who's not very well.

TAKE ME OUT

A panel of women hire a contract killer to assassinate Paddy McGuinness.

BIG BROTHER, WHERE ART THOU?

A Coen brothers re-make of TV's greatest non-event, starring Steve Buscemi as Davina McCall.

Next season: DESPERATE HOUSEMATES

Still in development:-

PETER AND JORDAN SING PETER AND GORDON

The celebrity ex-couple cover *A World Without Love* but a row breaks out when they reach the line 'Birds sing out of tune'.

GLOSSARY OF TERMS

PRE-SIG: the good bit they stick on the front of a programme, before the signature tune, to lure viewers into thinking the show's going to be better than it is.

POST-SIG: the rubbish bit they stick on the end, after the credits, in the hope that no one will see it.

(Clearly, the latter does not apply in the case of this book.)

SLIGHTLY SELECTIVE INDEX

STEELE, DAVID, disgruntled chorister, 77, 97, 161

STEVENSON, JEFF, new breed warm-up, 153

STEWART, ED, 'Stewpot', 117

STUART, VIVIEN, 'toffee-nosed cow', said D. Jarman, 63

SUCHET, DAVID, played Larry Hart on radio, 198

SWANSON, GLORIA, *Sunset Boulevard*, 130

TAGONISTIC, ANN, red dwarf, had to plug headphones in herself, 62-3

TARBUCK, JIMMY, two words, 203-4

TAYLOR, EDWARD, AHLER, not Mahler, 65

THATCHER, MARGARET, Hurricane Hilda, 9, 22, 35, 43, 55, 76, 104, 135, 204

THATCHER, MARK, 'prat flap', 161

THOMPSON, EMMA, only appearance, 105

THORNTON, FRANK, bloody students, 207-8

TILES, ZENA, boyfriend, 192

TODD, BOB, in the name of, 181

TOOK, BARRY, heavyweight, 67-8

TORME, MEL, cummerbund, 195

TOWNSHEND, PETE, in the gents, 173

TRAVIS, DAVE LEE, Perkins, 117, 119

TREE, HERBERT BEERBOHM, wooden actor, 145

Still available, for some reason…

READY STEADY CROOK

by

BOB SINFIELD   &   TOM POOLE

(WANTED FOR CRIMES AGAINST
HUMOUR)

Join Scotland Yard's worst detectives,
Flint and Bone, as they blunder from
one grisly murder to the next.   An
insufficiently brief extract follows.

Published by
DOCTOR SIN UK

To order, please visit
www.lulu.com

Chapter One: HANDLE WITH CARE

Scene of the crime: an ordinary suburban street containing an ordinary block of mansion flats. On the ordinary first floor, an ordinary old lady is making tea in her ordinary kitchen when suddenly, she notices something ...um, extraordinary.

*   *

TRANSCRIPT OF INTERCOM EXCHANGE FROM DUTY OFFICE LOG AT PORTICO MANSIONS, SE1. TIMED AT 07:56, TUESDAY MAY 14TH.

MRS GRIMPEN
[RESIDENT]:   Mr Proctor?   Mr
                   Proctor!   It's
                   Mrs Grimpen in
                   Flat 7.

REGINALD
PROCTOR
[MANSIONS
CARETAKER]:   Eh?

MRS G: You'll have to
                   speak up, dear.
                   I'm deaf.

244

PROCTOR: I said, "eh?".

MRS G: I said, "I'm deaf".

PROCTOR: Righto, Mrs G.   Was there
         anything else?

MRS G: Eh?   Oh yes.   I've got
         something coming through
         my ceiling.   I...I think
         it's blood.   Hallo?   You
         a bit deaf, dear? I said...

         [CONVERSATION ENDS]

         *   *

By the time Sergeant Bone and I arrived at the
scene, a full forensic investigation was under way.
One Adrian Carmody, the old girl's upstairs
neighbour, had apparently been stabbed in the
comfort of his own flat. Bertha Machin MD, a red-
faced, tweedy woman, was giving the corpse the
once-over in between striking garish poses for the
Yard's photographer. Machin was new to us, up
from the country - and judging by her fingernails, it
seemed she'd brought most of it with her.   I
introduced myself. "Doctor, I'm Inspector Flint and
this is Sergeant Bone. What can you tell us?"

"Flint and Bone, eh? Sound like a couple of hard men!!"

The good doctor dissolved into girlish sniggers at her own 'joke'. To my left, I caught sight of Sergeant Bone attempting to join in. One of my sharper glances quickly put paid to that. "Is it extra for the cabaret, Doctor?" I enquired, satirically. "Perhaps, between houses, you'd care to tell us how and when Mr Carmody died."

"Last night about eleven, I'd say. Need some more tests to be accurate. A stab wound to the abdomen punctured his kidney and liver." To my relief, the medic was starting to sound like a professional...until she said, "Offal business!!" and resumed giggling like the short one out of The Krankies. Pausing only to point out that perhaps she shouldn't sell the scalpels just yet, I leant forward to get a closer look at the body. Annoyingly, Bone did the same.

"Crikey, sir!" he exclaimed. Does anyone still use words like 'crikey' apart from this time-warped Welshman? "Whoever did it must be pretty strong to push the knife right through like that."

"It wasn't pushed right through, Sergeant," Machin corrected him. "He was stabbed with the handle." She was right. Carmody, a good-looking, elegant man in his thirties, lay there immaculately dressed save for one small detail: a large knife protruding from his abdomen...blade out! Whoever did it must have held the knife by the blade.

"They must have hands like a rhinoceros!" I observed.

"A rhinoceros hasn't got hands, sir. Just four feet." Bone had failed to spot my use of a simile. Rather than embark on what would inevitably have been a pointless explanation, I told him to stay with Coco the Quack and get a statement from the caretaker while I quizzed the old dear who'd reported the crime. A natter with a rambling, senile pensioner promised much-needed relief from the forensic funster and my defective sergeant.

*   *

"Will it come out, do you think, Inspector?"

Mrs Grimpen and I were studying the blood-soaked area. I gave her the benefit of my professional opinion. "The only thing for bloodstains really is soaking in cold water."

"The ceiling?"

I was forced to admit that could be tricky. "You could always paint it red."

"Wouldn't think one man could make so much

mess, eh?" She seemed to be taking the catastrophe in her stride. "Go and sit in the parlour, dear. I'll bring your tea." I gladly did as she offered. The 'parlour' was musty, cob-webbed and claustrophobically decorated, but at least there wasn't blood all over the ceiling. My eyes went straight to a gaudy, yellowing cabaret poster on the far wall, depicting a grinning man with sugar-and-water hair, sporting a waxed moustache and holding a dagger. Beneath him, in gothic print, ran the legend, 'The Great Grimaldi'. So eye-catching was this that it took me a moment to realise one of the clunky armchairs was occupied. A fat old man sat staring into the distance, seemingly oblivious of my presence, just as I'd been of his.

"I beg your pardon, sir. I didn't know there was anyone else here." Silence. I tried another conversational tack. "My word, what a splendid poster, eh? The Great Grimaldi. Are you a fan, sir?" Perhaps he was deaf. "I SAID, ARE YOU A..."

"Tea up, Inspector." Mrs Grimpen arrived with a raffia tray.

"Mrs Grimpen, your friend here...is he a bit deaf?"

"No dear, he's a bit dead." As she put the

tray down, one of the old man's eyes fell out. "Uncle Biffo's been gone for years. Couldn't bear to be without him, so we had him stuffed. They did a very bad job on his eyes though. That one's always coming out." She picked it up and re-inserted it in the empty socket. I sat down.

"<u>We</u> had him stuffed?" I questioned her use of the plural tense.

"Me and Tiddles. You're sitting on her." I stood up again. "I lost her a year ago." This appeared to upset Mrs G far more than the homicidal incident of the previous night. "The usual cat ailment."

"Feline flu?"

"Run over by a milk float. So I had her stuffed and all. Now we three can sit round the fireplace together, just like old times." I shot a glance at the fireplace just to make sure she hadn't had that stuffed too.

"How well did you know Mr Carmody upstairs?"

"Oh him!" The old girl returned to the matter in hand with some reluctance. "Hardly at all. Kept himself to himself, except..."

"Except...?"

"Well, sometimes I had to go up about the noise. Don't like to say really. He...had a lot of lady friends, you know...that sort of noise. Entertaining."

"I'm sure it was."

"No, he was entertaining them. I couldn't sleep."

"Neither could they, presumably." I asked her if there'd been any other kind of noise the night before. "Any arguments?"

"Not last night, but there was a bit of a kefuffle yesterday morning. Mr C was having a real set-to with old Jen, out in the street."

"Old Jen?" I braced myself for far-fetched tales of yet another stuffed person, but it emerged that Jen the Pen, as Mrs Grimpen described her, was a local down-and-out. I was struck by the curious name. "Jen the Pen? Some sort of writer before she took to the road?"

"Oh no, Inspector," she laughed. "Rhyming slang: pen and ink, stink. When she gets nervous, Jen has trouble controlling her...air flow. That's why I missed their row. I didn't dare open the window."

"Very wise." My cup of tea was untouched. For some reason, it seemed a tad unappetising. It was time to go, but on my way to the door, I pulled that 'one last thing' routine which always seemed to work for Columbo. "That poster..."

"Eh?" She seemed flustered. Fuck me, it did work!

"The Great Grimaldi. From a showbusiness family, are you?"

"Er...ooh no! No, never, that er...belonged to Tiddles...I mean, Uncle Biffo."

Clearly, I'd hit on something, though at this stage I'd no idea what. "Very decorative anyway. Now if you think of anything else, you'll get straight through to me on this number."

I fished a card out of my wallet and handed it over. She squinted at the small print. "What, at Miss Whip's School of Discipline?" Shit, wrong card.

"That must belong to..." I invented someone quickly, "...my wife." She gawped at me. "I'll see myself out."

*　　　　　　　*

STATEMENT BY REGINALD SEARCY
PROCTOR, TAKEN BY DS BRIAN BONE

Well, thing is, I had been in my
flat all night style of thing
when old Mrs G come through on
the squawk-box in the morning,

hollering at the top of her stairs about being deaf. I thought no more of it, as you do, then she said summit about blood coming through her ceiling style of thing. I said I'd be up in two ticks and it was blood all right, no mistaking it. I told her I seen a lot of it in Korea and she said yes, she knew them package tours could be rough. I said no, in 1952: commando! Anyhow, I said best call you lot, boys in blue style of thing as it was my guess there was summit bleeding up there. Either that or her ceiling was stigmatic. She said no, it was artex. I went up to take a look and she called after me to be careful but I said a commando never forgets his training. I mean, granted the muscles may have gone a bit but the brain's as sharp as a lemon.

I used me keys to gain entrance as there was no reply and opened the kitchen door to find some body in there. The body in there was Mr Carmody, the dentist. He was kneeling in a pool of blood. I think it was his. I remembered my commando training and screamed…I mean,

```
raised  the  alarm.   I  was  in  a
state of being shocked as Mr C was
a decent bloke what never harmed a
soul   outside   of   his   dental
practice, though he was a bit of a
boy know what I mean eh?  I mean,
phwoar!   Eh?   How  should  I  know
how  you  spell  it? P-H-W-O-A-R  I
suppose.  God help us, they don't
teach you coppers much these days,
do they?
```

*   *

"Stuffed, eh? Don't think I'd like that. Not dignified, see."

"Oh I don't know, Bone. A trip to the taxidermists might do you good. The departmental biscuits would last a lot longer."

We were back at the Yard, in the horribly cramped office I'm forced to share with Bone and our clerical assistant, Alice Blaize. As usual, she was out, so that was one good thing.

"I suppose you've got to make allowances for old age, sir."

Bone's attitude sickened me. I was not about to make allowances for pension book-wielding time-servers dithering about, covered in wrinkles and listening to *Friday Night is Music Night*. "Boil 'em down for glue, I say!"

"Sir you won't feel like that when you're old yourself."

"I won't let myself get into that state in the first place." I treated the sergeant to a close-up of my well-preserved complexion. "Look at that skin, Bone. I've been told I look late twenties." He muttered some remark about that being when I was born...which it wasn't. *"Adonis Vital Spark* tablets," I revealed my secret. "They stimulate the hormones. Talking of which, where's our beloved secretary today? Having another day off, I suppose, with an attack of 'wimmin's trouble'."

Bone winced. "Sir, don't be so coy. There is a name for it, you know."

"All right then, shopping."

"Alice will be in soon." He took on a protective air when mentioning her which I found deeply irritating. "She's at the dentist."

"What, having her fangs sharpened?" Nice one, Duncan!

"Sir, you're just saying that because she spurned your advances."

I wasn't having that. "Bone, if a man like me was to show the remotest interest in her, she'd be all over me like a rash. Power, that's what they go for - and looks!" At this point, I heard the door open but didn't bother to look round: I was on a roll. "Oh yes, if I were to lower my standards to the basement, I could have her anytime. Women are not my problem."

"More like the other way round!" That carping, 'estuary' accent could only belong to the shamen of shorthand herself.

"Ah Miss Blaize, we were just discussing your good points. Not a long conversation. How was the dentist? Excruciatingly painful?"

"Just a check-up, thank you, <u>Mister</u> Flint." Alice always made a point of failing to address me as 'Inspector', partly because of her civilian status, but mostly to piss me off. Naturally, I didn't fall for it. I mean, why should something as petty as that get to me? The very idea. As if that could rile me in any way whatsoever. Cow!! I decided to exclude her from the conversation by returning to police matters.

"Bone, did you get anything from...?"

"Oh Alice, I brought you some more *Spot the Difference* forms." My junior officer was as attentive as ever. Sadly, he was attentive to her, not me.

"That's sweet of you, Brian. Thanks." She took what seemed to be a mountain of cereal packet cuttings from the lovesick sergeant with a gushing kind of gratitude which I found totally transparent but the witless Brian was unable to see through.

"Bone, I'm talking to you!"

"Mmm? Sorry, sir?" He seemed only vaguely aware of my presence.

"Pull yourself together, man. One flash of her teeth and you look like a haunted halibut!"

"You could do worse than take a leaf out of Brian's book when it comes to dealing with people." That was a bit rich, coming from her.

"Miss Blaize, Brian hasn't got a book: it's a pamphlet. Now Bone, did you get anything out of that caretaker?" Returning from Planet Alice, Bone showed me the statement. "Ah, so Carmody was something of a ladies' man, eh?"

"Yes sir, apparently he had quite a few sexual armadillos."

"Peccadillos!"

He then spent several minutes trying to convince me that a peccadillo was a South American ant-eater before revealing that he'd found the dead man's diary behind a chest of drawers. "The name Linda crops up all the time, sir. She was supposed to meet him last night at ten, around the time of death."

"It was ten, was it? So the unspeakable doctor finally came up with the goods, then."

"Only after she'd done a ventriloquist act with the corpse."

"That's horrid!" Miss Blaize chimed in.

"Bone, if ever I'm injured and Machin's at hand, shoot me."

"Why wait?"

"Thanks, Alice. Now Bone, have you got the name of this Linda woman?"

"I told you, sir. It's Linda."

Patience, Duncan, patience. "The _full_ name?"

"Oh, Linda McVane, it's circled here in red. Lives in Pimlico."

"Miss Blaize, run Linda McVane through the computer and send the results straight to the car. I think we'll drop in on her for a surprise chat. Oh and while you're about it, get the local plods to pick up an old dosser called Jen the Pen."

"Old Jen?" Bone piped up.

"You know her?"

"Everyone knows old Jen, sir. But she wouldn't have done it: she doesn't need a knife to commit murder, not with her bowels."

"So I hear. When she's nervous, right?"

"Aye, and it doesn't take much!"

"Best get her in anyway. Alice, tell them to use kid gloves."

"Sounds like they'll need rubber ones."

$*$ $*$

<u>REPORT BY WPC CHEGWIN ON THE APPREHENSION OF SUSPECT JENNIFER CLOTWORTHY A.K.A "JEN THE PEN"</u>:-

Suspect sighted in Inglethorpe Terrace at approximately 13:50 on Tuesday 14/5, retrieving a discarded can of Red Bull from a residential wheely bin. Approached suspect with caution as directed. On making contact, witnessed suspect expel contents of can and complain of the presence therein of a cigarette butt. "Some people are disgusting", she said. My colleague PC Fentiman then asked suspect to leave bins alone and accompany us to see DI Flint down at the Yard for a little word. At this point, suspect became hysterical in an anally obnoxious manner and shouted, "What you nicking me for? I ain't effing black."

With some difficulty and meeting with much resistance, PC Fentiman and I propelled suspect into rear of squad car and made straight for HQ, pausing every

twenty yards or so to get out and
wave doors about a bit.

＊　　　　　　　　＊

Bone rang the bell of her Dolphin Square flat and soon after, the breathtaking Linda appeared. Not that I was entranced at all. "Mrs McVane? We're from Scotland Yard." See? Perfectly in control.

"I only give to Oxfam" was all we heard before the door was shut in our faces. I nodded to Bone to ring again. He misinterpreted the gesture and started to leave. I pulled him back and rang the bell myself. This time it was opened with an air of impatience.

"We're police officers, madam. We'd like a word inside if you don't mind. It's rather delicate."

She eyed us coolly. "Have you any identification?" I fished a card out of my wallet and handed it over. Luckily, it wasn't from Miss Whip's School of Discipline. She raised an eyebrow, magnificently. "So, you're a member of the Dennis the Menace Fan Club." She gestured at Bone. "Who's this? Gnasher?"

© BOB SINFIELD & TOM POOLE 2008

Also out now, the sequel…

SIMPLY DEAD

by

BOB SINFIELD
& TOM POOLE

It's murder in Llandudno! DI Flint is
plunged into a Welsh web of intrigue
involving sex, drugs and OAP
karaoke nights with a Mick Hucknall
lookalike and a seagull shot at point-
blank range.

Published by
DOCTOR SIN UK

Now available on two CDs…

ENGLANDᴛʜᴇɪʀENGLAND

A full-cast dramatisation of
A.G. MacDonell's classic novel

Narrated by LESLIE PHILLIPS

Young Donald Cameron tours the country, collecting material for his book about the English and their curious habits. He gets involved in many comic set pieces, encountering that wonderful invention, the country house weekend party and, most famously, a hilarious village cricket match.

"A splendid narration. Leslie Phillips is superb." THE TIMES

To order, please contact:-

doctorsinuk@yahoo.co.uk